—*THE*—

NEW ROAD

TO

SERFDOM

"In this fiercely argued little book, Daniel Hannan calls on all Americans who love their country not to let Barack Obama take us down the road to European socialism. To do so would fulfill F. A. Hayek's warning that the overweening power of the state will reduce us all to serfdom. Hannan should know—as a prominent British conservative and a member of the European Parliament, his present resembles our future. Every patriotic American needs to read Hannan's urgent letter of warning to the nation."

—SEAN HANNITY

"*The New Road to Serfdom* provides an exquisitely clear insight into what makes America exceptional. This work strikingly renews F. A. Hayek's warning that centralized power leads to serfdom. Hannan writes to make us aware that the threat of serfdom did not end in the eighties or nineties with Thatcher, Reagan, or the Contract with America. We are still facing this threat, through policy and law that refute American values, freedom, and religiosity. This book calls on Americans to be grateful for the nation we have the privilege to belong to."

—NEWT GINGRICH

"Dan Hannan is a voice in the wilderness in Europe, crying out against state tyranny. But to us in America, he is a modern-day Paul Revere, warning us that socialism is coming and calling on us to battle against Obama's plans in order to save our freedom."

—DICK MORRIS, AUTHOR OF *Revolt!: How to Defeat Obama and Repeal His Socialist Programs*

"Daniel Hannan, a British patriot and friend of America, has reminded us of our unique good fortune as citizens of this exceptional republic. He has warned us of the dangers ahead, if we follow the European path. We should listen to him."

—*National Review*

"Hannan writes in snappy prose that frames difficult political propositions in nice anecdotal pictures."

—*New Criterion*

"An important book that spells out the dangers, brilliantly summarizes the state of play, and shows exactly why the American Constitution both deserves and needs protection from the new ruling class. . . . Hannan utters a passionate plea to the American people, as the last representatives of the freedoms for which the English-speaking people have given so many lives."

—*American Spectator*

"When Hannan speaks he's so eloquent he's almost mesmerizing . . . and he can write just as well as he can speak. Tightly written and readable, *The New Road to Serfdom* admires the United States and our governing document without drifting into starry-eyed idealism or unreasoned love. . . . It instead functions exactly as its subtitle suggests: a letter of warning to America. 'I am living in your future,' he writes. 'Let me tell you a few things about it.' We would do well to listen."

—*Dartmouth Review*

"As a call to Americans to reassert the virtues of federalism, decentralization, and individual liberty, *The New Road to Serfdom* is invaluable."

—*FrumForum*

—THE—
NEW ROAD
TO
SERFDOM

*A Letter of Warning
to America*

DANIEL HANNAN

BROADSIDE BOOKS
An Imprint of HarperCollinsPublishers
www.broadsidebooks.net

HarperCollins books may be purchased for educational, business, or sales promotional use. For information, please write: Special Markets Department, HarperCollins Publishers, 10 East 53rd Street, New York, NY 10022.

Broadside Books™ and the Broadside logo are trademarks of HarperCollins Publishers.

A hardcover edition of this book was published in 2010 by Harper, an imprint of HarperCollins Publishers.

FIRST BROADSIDE BOOKS PAPERBACK EDITION PUBLISHED 2011

Designed by Jaime Putorti

Library of Congress Cataloging-in-Publication Data has been applied for.

ISBN: 978-0-06-195694-2

11 12 13 14 15 OV/RRD 10 9 8 7 6 5 4 3 2 1

FOR SARA

The cause of America is, in a great measure, the cause of all mankind. Many circumstances have, and will arise, which are not local, but universal, and through which the principles of all lovers of mankind are affected, and in the event of which, their affections are interested.

—THOMAS PAINE,
COMMON SENSE, 1776

CONTENTS

ACKNOWLEDGMENTS

I am grateful to the many Americans who hosted me during the six months while I was writing this book: to Ed Feulner and Sally McNamara at the Heritage Foundation; to Fred Smith, Iain Murray, and Myron Ebell at the Competitive Enterprise Institute; to Michael Bowman and the American Legislative Exchange Council; to John Caldara of the Independence Institute; to John Goodman and Tab Boyles of the National Center for Policy Analysis; to Allen Roth and Jonah Goldberg; to Newt Gingrich and Dick Armey; and, most of all, to Lori Roman of Regular Folks United.

Thanks, too, to Adam Bellow for having had the idea in the first place, and to the brilliant David Batt, with whom, in many long conversations, I shaped my opinions into a semblance of order.

Thanks to my wonderful Scottish-American cousins in Philadelphia, John, Nancy, Mary, Ryan, and Lavina. And thanks especially to Annabel and Allegra, who have more patience than any father has the right to expect.

FOREWORD TO
THE PAPERBACK
EDITION

There's no getting around it: Barack Obama doesn't like Brits very much. Let's review the evidence. The president received from Gordon Brown a penholder made from the timbers of HMS *Gannet*, which had spent her life at sea prosecuting a successful war against the slave trade. He reciprocated with a set of DVDs.

In his first summit meeting with a British prime minister, he silkily downgraded the two countries' alliance. American presidents have to be careful with their superlatives, of course, lest they offend Canada or Israel or some other favored nation, yet previous U.S. leaders had no difficulty describing the United Kingdom as "our closest ally." George W. Bush cheerfully went further, calling the United Kingdom "our closest friend and strongest ally," and adding, on the day Baghdad fell in 2003, "America has no finer ally than Great Britain." For the forty-fourth president, however, Britain was simply "one of our allies," right up there with Bahrain and Honduras.

When an oil spill caused millions of dollars of damage in Louisiana and other parts of the Gulf littoral, President Obama used the occasion to attack an imaginary company called "British Petroleum." In fact, no such corporation had existed for a decade; it had become "BP" following a merger with Amoco, which gave it as many U.S. as British shareholders.

When George W. Bush met the Queen, he made a characteristic verbal slip and then, with an unrehearsed grin, remarked, "She gave me a look like only a mother could give a child." It was a touching phrase, a gracious acknowledgment of the United States's British heritage. His successor? His successor presented Her Majesty with an iPod loaded with . . . his own speeches.

Visiting West Africa for the first time, President Obama made a point of referring to the region's struggle for independence from Britain (not that it was much of a struggle; most African colonies were brought to self-government without a shot being fired in anger). Yet despite touring the slave stations, he managed to avoid any mention of the fact that the slave trade had been extirpated as a result of years of struggle by the Royal Navy.

Nor has the president acknowledged Britain's presence in Afghanistan in any major speech. Not once. All right, we may not have as many soldiers there as you have, but ours is easily the second-largest national contingent and, being stationed in the part of the country where the insurgency is fiercest, our soldiers have suffered a higher proportionate casualty rate than any others: 374 fatalities at the time of writing.

This goes beyond symbolism or etiquette. The present administration has come dangerously close to pressing the position of Peronist Argentina on the Falkland Islands. In a series of resolutions, it has lined up with such virulently anti-Western figures as Venezuela's Hugo Chavez and Nicaragua's Daniel Ortega to back Argentina's demands for negotiations on sovereignty. The state department has even taken to referring to the disputed territories by their Argentine name, Las Malvinas.

You might be thinking that an Anglophobic president is my problem rather than yours. But, my friends, it is your problem, too. Partly because it is never a good idea to alienate one's allies—and there has rarely been a worse time to be a traditional ally of the United States, as Poles and Czechs, Indians and Israelis will tell you. Mainly, though, it's your problem because Barack Obama's attitude toward Britain tells us a great deal about his attitude toward the United States.

Where does it come from, your president's distaste for my people? He once went on what sounds like a pretty ghastly bachelor party in a suburban part of my constituency, but that alone can't explain it. And he once sat next to a disagreeable Brit on a flight (an episode he describes at length in one of his books).

The conventional explanation is that he is bitter

about the way his grandfather Hussein Onyango Obama was interned during the Mau Mau rebellion, a partly tribal war in Kenya in the 1950s between pro-British and pro-independence factions. But this explanation doesn't fit with what Obama himself has written.

Barack never knew his grandfather, but what he later found out repelled him. Despite being detained by the British authorities, Onyango had remained something of an imperialist, believing that the British had earned their place in Kenya through superior organization. He even used to argue that Africans were too lazy to make a success of independence. The young Obama was horrified. "I had imagined him to be a man of his people, opposed to white rule," he wrote in *Dreams from My Father*. "What Granny [Sarah Obama, one of Onyango's wives] had told me scrambled that image completely, causing ugly words to flash across my mind. Uncle Tom. Collaborator. House nigger."

No, the president's antipathy comes not from the grandfather he disdained, but from the father he worshipped—albeit from a distance. Barack Obama Senior abandoned Obama's mother and had almost nothing to do with the young Barry (as he was known throughout his childhood and adolescence). He did, however, make one journey to Hawaii, which had an enormous impact on the ten-year-old future president. Barry, as boys sometimes do, had been telling tall tales about his absent father. He had implied to his classmates that Barack Senior was a great chief, and that he would himself one day inherit the tribal leadership. He was mortified when his class teacher asked his father to talk to the class, fearing that his fibs would be exposed. His anxieties vanished as the handsome Kenyan strode into the room in African dress, and proceeded to give a talk that was the defining moment of Barry's childhood:

> *He was leaning against Miss Hefty's thick oak desk and describing the deep gash in the earth where mankind had first appeared. He spoke of the wild animals that still roamed the plains, the tribes that still required a young boy to kill a lion to prove his manhood. He spoke of the customs of the Luo, how elders received the utmost respect and made laws for all to follow under great-trunked trees. And he told us of Kenya's struggle to be free, how the British had wanted to stay and unjustly rule the people, just as they had in America; how many had been enslaved only because of the color of their skin, just as they had in America, but that Kenyans, like all of us in the room, longed to be free and develop themselves through hard work and sacrifice.*

That view of a constant struggle by the oppressed against the oppressors, the colonies against the colonizers, the have-nots against the haves, became the mainstay of Barack Junior's worldview. In *The Roots of*

Obama's Rage, Dinesh D'Souza argues that Obama's domestic and foreign policy agendas are inspired by his father's 1950s anti-colonialism. The mistake that every other analyst has made, argues D'Souza, is to try to fit Obama into America's racial narrative. But the battle for civil rights is only tangentially a part of his story. Indeed, he has infuriated many black political organizations by refusing to take up the issues that they care about, such as the minimum wage and affirmative action. His struggle was not that against segregation in Mississippi but that of African protectorates against European empires.

For example, Obama's climate change policies make little sense either as an attempt to slow global warming or as a way to make the United States more popular. But they make perfect sense as a mechanism for the redistribution of wealth from rich nations to poor. (D'Souza notes, as an instance, the way in which the Obama administration has banned offshore drilling in the United States while sponsoring it in Brazil). The same is true of his enthusiasm for nuclear disarmament. It seems bizarre to be pursuing the elimination of atomic weapons in a forum that doesn't include Iran or North Korea. But, argues D'Souza, this isn't really about Iran or North Korea. It's about making America a less warlike, less intimidating, less—in a word—*imperial* nation.

In disdaining Britain, the president also disdains

the things that Britain bequeathed to the thirteen colonies and, through them, to the American republic: the common law, a peculiar emphasis on personal freedom and property rights, distrust of government, a determination that laws should not be made, nor taxes levied, save by elected representatives.

These things, as we shall see, have an ancient lineage. The founders were drawing, consciously and openly, on a patrimony that they traced back to the English Civil War or even further. To the anti-colonialist mind-set, however, there was nothing especially laudable about this patrimony. The main recommendation of the early patriots to Obama was not that they preached a set of sublime political ideals, but that they could be portrayed, after a fashion, as anti-colonialists. He stressed this theme in his Inauguration Day address: "In the year of America's birth, in the coldest of months, a small band of patriots huddled by dying campfires on the shores of an icy river. The capital was abandoned. The enemy was advancing. The snow was stained with blood. . . ." He repeated it in a number of visits to developing nations. When the Arab revolts erupted in 2011, he compared the demonstrators to the Boston Tea Partiers—a compliment he has never paid to the actual anti-tax movements in the United States.

The idea that the early patriot leaders were also upholding an inheritance—that they were as much conservatives as radicals—doesn't fit this portrayal. But, as we shall see, the founders constantly argued that they were simply defending their birthright—a birthright that has exalted your country above the run of nations. Accepting this truth, however, means accepting the special place of the men who made the republic. It means accepting that the United States is not just a multiculti fusion that owes as much to Ruthenian immigrants and the Arapaho as it does to Washington, Franklin, and Jefferson. It means accepting that the United States is part of a wider family of English-speaking nations.

It is here that the president's dislike for Britain becomes your problem, too. Throughout the twentieth century, our two countries have been close associates, if not always formal allies. We fought side by side against the totalitarianisms of the modern age: fascism, communism, Islamic fundamentalism. Even when we didn't formally take up arms in a common cause, no one doubted our common sympathy. The British government tacitly backed the United States in its war against Spain in 1898, and the U.S. government quietly returned the favor two years later during the South African war. Our two countries fought together in the two world wars, in Korea, in Iraq, and in Afghanistan. Only once, during the Suez crisis, did the relationship break down—with, as it was to turn out, calamitous results. (Eisenhower later called his failure to back Britain's military action against Gamal Abdel Nasser his "greatest regret.")

When Argentina invaded the Falkland Islands,

Ronald Reagan was in no doubt as to who his friends were. He instructed the Defense Department to make available any matériel that the British needed. Indeed, he went about as far as a benevolent neutral can go without formally opening hostilities, offering intelligence and logistical support to the United Kingdom.

Where Reagan saw an English-speaking democracy threatened by a dictatorship, Obama seems to see an imperial relic. Yet if the Falkland Islands are an imperial relic, a territory that just happened to be settled by English speakers with a stubborn attachment to personal freedom and parliamentary rule, what is the United States? The founders grew up with a strong sense that they were the heirs and guardians of a series of defined British freedoms. When they saw those freedoms arbitrarily withheld by a remote monarchy, they took to the battlefield to assert their rights. The liberties that those patriot leaders believed they had won by inheritance were then encoded in a new constitutional dispensation. That is the essence of American exceptionalism—the exceptionalism whose very existence the current president seems not to accept.

The argument of this book is that the U.S. Constitution is a unique document, and that its tenets have served to keep your country prosperous and free; that the United States has now become the surest repository for the freedoms that my own country once took for granted but has let slip; and that your rulers are now rushing to dismantle your constitutional settlement. If they succeed, the United States will become a lot more like other places: more highly taxed, more heavily regulated, more centralized, less confident, poorer, weaker.

When Barack Obama sent back the bust of Winston Churchill that had stood in the White House, he wasn't simply repudiating the man who, as prime minister, had defended the British Empire. He was also repudiating the foremost advocate of the idea that the Anglosphere nations have a special dream and a special task: that it is our duty, when others falter, to defend individual liberty, parliamentary supremacy, and the rule of law.

Fail in that duty, and we don't simply make the world a darker place; we spurn our fathers, and we disinherit our children.

> The support of the State governments in all their rights,
> as the most competent administrations for our domestic
> concerns and the surest bulwarks against anti-republican
> tendencies; economy in the public expense, that labor
> may be lightly burthened; the honest payment of our
> debts and sacred preservation of the public faith; freedom
> of religion; freedom of the press, and freedom of person
> under the protection of the habeas corpus, and trial by
> juries impartially selected. These principles form the
> bright constellation which has gone before us and guided
> our steps through an age of revolution and reformation.
> The wisdom of our sages and blood of our heroes have
> been devoted to their attainment.
>
> —THOMAS JEFFERSON, 1800

American self-belief is like a force of nature, awesome and inexorable. It turned a dream of liberty into a functioning nation, and placed that nation's flag on the moon. It drew settlers across the seas in the tens of millions, and liberated hundreds of millions more from the evils of fascism and communism. If it has occasionally led the United States into errors, they have tended to be errors of exuberance. On the whole, the world has reason to be thankful for it.

Every visitor is struck, sooner or later, by the confidence that infuses America. It is written in people's faces. Even the poorest immigrants rarely have the pinched look that dispossessed people wear on other continents. Instead, they seem buoyant, energetic, convinced that, when they finish their night classes, they will be sitting where you sit in your suit.

I felt the pulse of American optimism even as a young child, though I had no words for it. My uncle had moved to Philadelphia from a village in the west of Scotland. He never lost his accent and was known to the end of his days as "Scotty" in the bars of north Philly. Yet he seemed to have lost all traces of the self-consciousness that Scots usually recognize in one another. He had somehow grown into his adopted country, becoming commensurately cheerful and expansive and confident and loud.

When I was eighteen, I spent two months meandering slowly down the Mississippi from Chicago to New Orleans with a college friend. Afterward, we traveled across the South, lingering for several days in Birmingham, Alabama, for no better reason, as I recall, than that we liked the Lynyrd Skynyrd song about it. Before flying home, we were (as was traditional in those pre-Giuliani days) mugged in New York City. We felt we had savored a measure of the diversity of American life. And, beneath the superficial differences, we kept finding the same character traits: enthusiasm, artlessness, impatience, optimism.

Only much later did it occur to me that these are not innate characteristics. Every American, after all, must at some stage have arrived from somewhere else and, like my uncle, shed an earlier identity. American optimism is not a genetic condition, but a product of particular circumstances.

The air of the new world can work even on the casual visitor. When I write about my own country's politics, I'm as cynical as the next world-weary Brit. But, whenever I go to Washington, I give in to the guileless enthusiasm that foreigners so often dismiss as naïveté. Like James Stewart's character in *Mr. Smith Goes to Washington*, I goggle reverently at the Lincoln and Jefferson memorials, "The Battle Hymn of the Republic" swelling in my mind.

At least I used to. On my most recent visit, as I stood before the statue of your third president, I fancied I heard a clanking noise. Doubtless it was Jefferson's shade rattling his chains in protest at what is being done to his country. The ideals for which he had fought, and which he had incorporated into the founding texts of the republic—freedom, self-reliance, limited government, the dispersal of power—are being forgotten. The characteristics that once set America apart are being eliminated. The United States is becoming just another country.

To put it another way, the self-belief is waning. Americans, or at least their leaders, no longer seem especially proud of their national particularisms. The qualities that make America unique—from federalism to unrestricted capitalism, from jealousy about sovereignty to willingness to maintain a global military presence—now appear to make America's spokesmen embarrassed.

One by one, the differences are being ironed out. The United States is Europeanizing its health system, its tax take, its day care, its welfare rules, its approach to global warming, its foreign policy, its federal structure, its unemployment rate. Perhaps Americans are keen to fit in. Perhaps they feel awkward about being the odd man out.

I'm struck by how many American liberals now seem to see their country through European eyes. You are especially likely to meet these embarrassed Americans—understandably enough, I suppose—in Europe, where they are keen to impress on you that they never voted for George Bush.

"We don't have anything like this in the States," they say wonderingly, over and over again. A middle-aged lady from Jersey City with whom I spent an afternoon in the French Basque country repeated the line so often that, after a while, I snapped and retorted, "Yes you do: They're called restaurants, for heaven's sake."

For years, some Europeans have clutched at enduring myths about Americans. Fair enough, you might say: All peoples stereotype each other. The new and unsettling development is how many American lefties have started to believe these myths about themselves.

I have a young cousin from Colorado: a clever, charming, beautiful girl. Like most first-time voters, she enthusiastically backed Barack Obama. Among the many hopes she had for him was that he would make the United States more popular by bringing it into line with other countries.

But here's the thing: Despite having studied and traveled in Europe, she has a number of fixed ideas about the difference between the Old and New Worlds. She is convinced, for example, that Europeans are politer than Americans. Lots of Americans think this, and it's very flattering. But, believe me, it is utter rot. Americans come across to us as courtly and prim, careful to avoid bad language, punctilious about using correct titles, almost never drunk in public. How anyone can visit, say, Paris and come back thinking that Europeans are unusually well-mannered is beyond me. My cousin sort of knows all this. But she still likes to cling to her image of the boorish Yank, even if she rarely sees it actualized.

While we're about it, let's explore a few more of these *idées fixes*.

"Americans know nothing of the world: most of them don't even have passports."
International travel is, of course, partly a function of geography: the distance from Los Angeles to Miami is the same as that from London to Baku. But there are plenty of Europeans who

rarely travel. It's just that, for some reason, the stay-at-home tendencies of the peasant farmer in Calabria or Aragon are treated as a national treasure rather than a sign of parochialism.

"America is a young country. It has no history."
In fact, the United States is older than virtually every country in Europe. Most European states have drawn up their constitutions since 1945. Several didn't exist as nation-states at all until after World War I. Even Germany and Italy, as political entities, date only from the late nineteenth century. The extraordinary longevity of the U.S. Constitution is eloquent tribute to the success of America's political model.

"Americans are great polluters: they're addicted to their cars."
Cars, too, are a function of geography—and, indeed, of history. The United States is spacious; its land is cheap; its towns were generally built after the invention of the automobile, and therefore without the narrow streets that characterize European villages. These factors have made Argentines, Australians, and South Africans every bit as addicted to their cars as Americans. And, indeed, despite punitive taxation, congested roads, and a broad range of alternatives, Europe-

ans, too, seem to like driving: hence the number of coercive policies needed to stop them.

"The United States is a country of endless suburbs."
Yes, and very pleasant they are. You couldn't say the same of the tower-blocks that ring most French, Dutch, or Belgian cities, seething with angry immigrants. Indeed, when French politicians want to euphemize the issues of street crime and social breakdown, they call it *le problème des banlieues*: "the suburb problem."

"Americans have no culture. Where is their Shakespeare?"
America's Shakespeare, obviously, is Shakespeare. Since he died four years before the *Mayflower* set sail, he is surely just as much the property of those Englishmen who carried his works to new lands as of those who stayed behind. If we look at more recent history, I'd have thought a canon that includes Ralph Waldo Emerson and Mark Twain, Emily Dickinson and John Steinbeck, F. Scott Fitzgerald and Ernest Hemingway, can hold its own against most comers.

"Americans are in love with guns. Their society is crime-ridden."
Certainly there are more guns in the United

States than in Europe (except freedom-loving Switzerland). And, yes, that imbalance has an impact on crime figures, both positively and negatively. The U.S. states that have the laxest gun laws have more homicides, but many fewer burglaries and muggings: Criminals, like the rest of us, are capable of making risk assessments. Why is it, though, that when a disturbed American teenager murders his classmates, it is invariably described as "another example of America's love affair with the gun," whereas when the same thing happens in, say, Finland, it is simply a tragedy from which it would be insensitive to draw political conclusions?

"American TV is trash."
Oh, come *on*. The world watches U.S. television, from *The Sopranos* to *The Simpsons*. If you want truly abominable television, try the diet of game shows and soaps served up across much of southern Europe. How anyone can watch Italian TV, and then claim with a straight face that American programming is junk, completely defeats me.

In fact, many of the evils that Europeans project onto the United States not only wrongly describe America but more accurately describe Europe. Consider the most common charge of all: the accusation that Americans, because of their low-tax low-welfare model, are heartless and greedy. In fact, Americans are measurably more generous than Europeans: The average American gives $300 a year to charity, the average European $80.

Stereotypes can be remarkably resistant to facts. When an earthquake hit Haiti in January 2010, European media loudly asked what was taking the Americans so long to respond. In fact, within hours of Port-au-Prince crumbling, the United States had sent an aircraft carrier with nineteen helicopters, hospital and assault ships, the 82nd Airborne Division with 3,500 troops, and hundreds of medical personnel, and had put the airport on an operational footing (or "established an occupation" as an angry French minister put it). And the EU? The EU had held a press conference, expressed its condolences, and gone back to congratulating itself on its moral superiority over the stingy Yanks.

I'm afraid most of us tend, subconsciously, to fit the facts to our opinions rather than the other way around. The present U.S. administration is doing everything it can to win over its detractors. President Obama has traced a cat's cradle of vapor around the planet, apologizing for American arrogance, pledging his support for carbon reductions and nuclear disarmament, signing up to supra-national conventions, even refashioning the United States' domestic arrangements to make them more European. As we shall see, while he is personally popular, none of these initiatives has served to pacify America's critics.

When the United States defeated Spain in 1898, the British poet Rudyard Kipling addressed a poem to the newest world power:

Take up the White Man's burden—
And reap his old reward:
The blame of those ye better,
The hate of those ye guard.

The burden is now a black man's, and every friend of America must wish him well. But don't expect thanks from those ye guard: That's not how human nature works.

A hundred years ago, my country was where yours is now: a superpower, admired and resented—sometimes, in a complex way, by the same people. We understand better than most that popularity is not bought through mimicry, but through confidence. You are respected, not when you copy your detractors, but when you outperform them.

Until very recently, the United States did this very well. While it may have drawn sneers from European intellectuals, denunciation from Latin American demagogues, violence from Middle Eastern radicals, the populations of all these parts of the world continued to try to migrate to the United States, and to import aspects of American culture to their own villages.

Now, though, American self-belief is on the wane. No longer are the political structures designed by the heroes of Philadelphia automatically regarded as guarantors of liberty. America is becoming less American, by which I mean less independent, less prosperous, and less free.

The character of the United States, more than of any other country on earth, is bound up with its institutions. The U.S. Constitution was both a product and a protector of American optimism. When one is disregarded, the other dwindles.

This book is addressed to the people of the United States on behalf of all those in other lands who, convinced patriots as they may be, nonetheless recognize that America stands for something. Your country actualizes an ideal. If you give up on that ideal, all of us will be left poorer.

— THE —
NEW ROAD
TO
SERFDOM

1

WHAT MAKES AMERICA DIFFERENT

There is a twofold liberty, natural (I mean as our nature is now corrupt) and civil or federal. The first is common to man with beasts and other creatures. By this, man as he stands in relation to man simply, hath liberty to do what he lists: it is a liberty to evil as well as to good. The other kind of liberty I call civil or federal; it may also be termed moral, in reference to the covenant between God and man, and the politic covenants and constitutions amongst men themselves. This liberty is the proper end and object of authority, and cannot subsist without it; and it is a liberty to that only which is good, just and honest.

–JOHN WINTHROP, 1645

America is different; different for the most basic of reasons. Most Americans owe their nationality to the fact that they, or their relatively recent ancestors, chose it.

This might sound obvious, even trite. But think about the implications. Other countries tend to be defined by territory, language, religion, or ethnicity. What makes someone Japanese or Ethiopian or Swedish? It comes down, in essence, to blood and soil. But Americans became Americans by signing up to a set of ideals. They were making an active choice to leave behind one way of life and to adopt another.

What characterizes that way of life? The answer has not changed very much over the centuries. It is the reply that the framers of the constitution would have given. It is little changed, indeed, from the explanation that would have been offered by the Puritans as they made their *hejira* across the Atlantic. The essence of America is freedom.

To the earliest settlers, freedom meant in the first place freedom of conscience: the ability to congregate and worship without coercion. But implied in this freedom is much else. John Milton, the contemporary and champion of those pilgrim leaders, understood that liberty in religious affairs was the securest basis for liberty in civil affairs. A society in which individuals regulated their own relations with the Almighty would tend, by nature, to be a society of sturdy and self-reliant citizens. If men were free to interpret the strictures of their Creator without intermediation, they would be equally assertive in politics. If congregations could elect their ministers, towns would expect to elect their magistrates.

It is important to be clear about one thing at the outset. Neither the earliest Americans nor their heirs saw liberty simply as an absence of rules. (This Milton called "license" and heartily disliked.) Liberty, for them, meant the virtuous application of informed judgment. Rather than an external discipline imposed by prelates and princes, their society would be governed by an internal discipline generated by personal morality. John Winthrop, who led the pilgrims to the New World, drew the distinction in the quotation that opens this chapter.

As long as this form of liberty was secure, government would be constantly improved by the free exchange of ideas: a marketplace of creeds in which, over time, the good ideas would drive out the bad ones. As Milton put it: "Opinion in good men is but knowledge in the making."

This philosophy was given concrete form in the earliest North American settlements. Distant as they were from their king, the colonists fell into the habit of organizing their affairs at an extremely local level. With neither an episcopacy nor an aristocracy on their continent, they took naturally to the idea of self-government. When the U.S. Constitution enshrined the principles of decentralization and representative government, it was simply reiterating the long-standing customs of most Americans.

To put it another way, the New World attracted those who sought freedom and independence. The conditions of the early settlements were conducive to these same values. So it is hardly surprising that these ideals should in time have been codified in the U.S. Constitution.

The United States is the realization of a libertarian archetype—both in theory and in practice. Its constitution, as we shall see, is unique in the emphasis it places on the individual rather than the government. And, unlike some constitutions, it is not simply an abstract or aspirational document. The freedoms it guarantees were very real to its framers and, by and large, have remained real to their successors.

Loyalty to the nation implies allegiance to these ideas. American patriotism is, at least in part, a political statement. This gives it a different timbre to other national loyalties, rooted as they are in place and race.

The Japanese, the Ethiopian, or the Swede might also be a convinced patriot, in the sense that he has a special affinity with his own state and its symbols. And so he should: It is proper and healthy to feel a particularly warm sentiment toward the land that shaped you. But there is, in this patriotism, something unconditional. These countries might be capitalist or socialist; they might be atheist or they might have state churches; they might be monarchies or republics; but they would still recognizably be the same countries. The United States is peculiar in that it is defined by the institutions of its government, and by the philosophy that they represent.

This doesn't mean that American patriotism is more valid than anyone else's. I love my own nation very dearly. I am never happier than when tramping its countryside. I admire the character of my people: brave, morose, taciturn, stoic, drunk, belligerent, indignant at injustice. My feelings have little to do with the political institutions of the United Kingdom. Indeed, as I shall explain later on, I think that there is a great deal wrong with how Britain is currently governed. But it wouldn't occur to me to live in another country simply because it was more congenially administered.

America, as I say, is different. Allegiance to the United States means allegiance to its foundational texts and the principles inherent therein. It means loyalty to the republican ideal: the ideal, that is, of a virtuous, independent, and freestanding citizenry. Those who reject these ideals, who eschew the principles on which the United States was founded, can fairly be described as un-American.

I know that many people, in the United States and abroad, detest that term, seeing it as intolerant, even McCarthyite. But it is important to remember that America has generally had a civic rather than an ethnic conception of citizenship. The label "un-American" is not affixed to, say, immigrant communities or religious minorities; it is applied to those who want to turn the United States into a fundamentally different country.

For the avoidance of doubt, the last thing I want to do is excuse McCarthyism. Senator McCarthy was a foul-mouthed bully, and many guiltless Americans suffered as a consequence of his ambitions. Nonetheless, it is worth remembering that the hunt for those guilty of un-American activities was prompted by genuine cases of Soviet espionage. High-ranking government officials had been secretly working for an enemy regime. Their aim, as they later cheerfully admitted, was wholly to transform their country, to wipe away nearly two hundred years of constitutional development and subject America to an alien ideology: communism. The term "un-American" was precisely apposite.

In the hysteria that followed, more innocent victims than traitors were condemned. Committed democrats, who simply happened to hold left-wing views, were treated as agents of a foreign power. Indeed, the ideological persecution that accompanied the search for communist agitators was itself rather un-American, negating as it did the belief in freedom of conscience that had motivated the early colonists. But this doesn't invalidate the notion that some positions can reasonably be classed as un-American, in that they are incompatible with the vision of the founders as upheld and developed by their successors.

Because the essence of America is doctrinal, rather than territorial or racial, people around the world tend to take up positions for or against it. You don't often hear of, say, anti-Colombianism. But anti-Americanism is the credo of those who loathe the values that were built into the bricks of the republic. Anti-Americans take many forms. They can be European intellectuals who see American capitalism as pitiless, crass, and vulgar. They can be Middle Eastern *jihadis* who fear the Americanization of their own societies. They can be Latin American *anti-yanquistas* whose hostility to U.S. foreign policy is laced with resentment against the émigrés who throw their dollars around when they return to their home pueblos. They can be apologists for African strongmen, or proponents of an autocratic "Asian way."

These disparate groups might disagree profoundly on what would constitute an ideal society. But they agree on what doesn't. They dislike free markets ("greed"). They dislike unrestrained consumerism ("vulgarity"). They dislike the assumption that all societies are capable of democratic development ("Yankee imperialism"). They dislike the idea that people should be free to choose a different lifestyle from their parents' ("coca-colonialism"). In short, they dislike liberty, and resent the country that most embodies it.

The flip side is that there are many more around the world who admire what America stands for, who see the country as a repository of freedom, who exult in its triumphs and regret its failures.

And, of course, there *are* failures. Like every nation on Earth, the United States can behave selfishly and hypocritically. It doesn't always live up to the ideals of its constitution. Indeed, the premise of this chapter needs some qualification. When I wrote that most Americans had consciously chosen their nationality, I might have added that not all were in this category. Some were incorporated into the growing republic when their homes were annexed from Mexico. Some were carried to the New World in bondage. Some had inhabited the continent for many thousands of years, and were never asked whether they wanted to be Americans.

There was, in other words, a gap between theory and practice. Not everyone who lived within the territory of the United States had the same opportunities. While successive governments did in time try to offer everyone the full dignities implied by U.S. citizenship, they sometimes failed. Then again, occasional failure is part of the human condition. To say that the American dream has not always been realized is no more than to say that perfection is not of this world.

This point is worth stressing, because critics of the United States, domestic and foreign, are never happier than when alleging double standards. It is sometimes argued, for example, that the achievements of the American republic are devalued by the fact that it had displaced an aboriginal culture. But how can we possibly quantify human happiness? Who can judge whether a Native American today, with access to education, medicine, and the full range of modern recreational technology, is better off than he would have been had Europeans never arrived in North America? Or whether, if his quality of life is indeed superior, that superiority justifies the terrible price paid by those of his kin who died as the result of unfamiliar pathogens or lost hunting grounds? And who can say what cost to the indigenous peoples is redeemed by America's contributions to human happiness, from the invention of the airplane to the defeat of Nazism?

I don't see how we can comfortably answer any of these questions. What we *can* say with some certainty is this: Having at times behaved very shabbily toward the earlier inhabitants of the continent, the U.S. authorities eventually tried to do the right thing, giving Native Americans a choice between assimilation and autonomy. This record compares favorably enough with other countries where settlers have supplanted less technologically advanced peoples. But, even if it didn't, it would in no sense cheapen either the motives or the achievements of those Americans who sought over the centuries, and with surprising success, to actualize the dream of a free, egalitarian, and open polity.

The same argument applies with regard to slavery. This needs to be said because, of all the weapons in the anti-American arsenal, the history of slavery is the one most worn with use. Make the argument that the American Constitution is a uniquely benign document that has served to keep an entire nation prosperous and free, and you will sooner or later be told that it was a slave-owners' charter that valued some human beings at three fifths of the worth of others.

There is, of course, some truth in this accusation, which was leveled at the time both by abolitionists in the United States and by British and American Tories who opposed the project of independence. "How is it that we hear the greatest yelps for liberty among the drivers of Negroes?" demanded the most eloquent British Tory of his generation, Dr. Johnson, in 1775.

Once again, though, it needs to be remembered that Man is fallen. There isn't a country on Earth that hasn't done things in the past that, viewed from the vantage of the present, are shameful. The fact that a nation doesn't always live up to its ideals, or justify its self-image, doesn't mock those ideals or invalidate that self-image. On the contrary, it can spur the nation to greater effort. And, in the case of slavery, this is more or less what happened.

It is perfectly legitimate, when discussing the U.S. Constitution and the vision of its authors, to draw attention to the persistence, first of slavery, then of codified racial segregation, and then of unofficial discrimination. Well into the 1950s, supporters of segregation, led by the veteran Georgia senator Richard

Russell, cited the Constitution and repeated Supreme Court decisions in support of their position. But it is only fair to give the full picture. If we want to bring up slavery, we must refer, also, to the anti-slavery campaign, and to the huge price its adherents were prepared to pay in pursuit of their objectives, including death on the battlefield. If we are determined to remember segregation, we should likewise recall the civil rights campaigners. If we want to discuss racism, we can hardly ignore the fact that, in 2008, Americans elected a mixed-race president.

American patriots, including those who didn't vote for Barack Obama, should nonetheless take pride in the fact that his victory in some measure wiped away the stain of slavery and segregation. Those who believe in collective sin must also accept the logic of collective redemption. If all Americans, including those who never owned slaves, were diminished by the fact that the institution survived for as long as it did, then all Americans, including those who voted for McCain, are elevated by the fact that they live in a country that has moved in the space of forty years from the formalized exclusion of black voters to the election of a black head of state.

Indeed, the worst losers in the 2008 presidential electorate were arguably the dinosaurs of the black power movement, who found that their narrative of race relations in America had been falsified overnight. It is no surprise that Jeremiah Wright and Jesse "I wanna cut his nuts off" Jackson seemed so determined to sabotage Barack Obama's presidential campaign. They understood that his election would put them out of business, spectacularly belying their main contention, namely that American democracy is closed to minorities, and that there are limits to how high an African American can rise.

———————

The election of Barack Obama gave America's external critics, too, a moment's pause. For the first year of his administration, some anti-Americans reexamined their prejudices. If a mixed race candidate who had opposed the Iraq war could be elected in Washington, perhaps America was not quite the sinister plutocracy they had imagined.

President Obama immediately set about reinforcing the idea that he was different from his forty-three predecessors, withdrawing foreign garrisons, signing up to a number of international conventions, committing America to climate change targets, and attempting a series of domestic reforms, above all in health care, aimed at making America more like Europe. We shall look at these policies in detail later on. For now it is enough to note that it didn't take long before the anti-Americans were playing their old tunes again.

"There isn't an American president since Eisenhower who hasn't ended up, at some point or other, being depicted by the world's cartoonists as a cowboy astride a phallic missile," prophesied David Aaronovitch in the London *Times* shortly before the 2008 election. "It happened to Bill Clinton when he bombed Iraq; it will happen to Mr. Obama when his reinforced forces in Afghanistan or Pakistan mistake a meeting of tribal elders for an unwise gathering of Taliban and al-Qaeda." It didn't take long for this prediction to be fulfilled. Before President Obama's first year was out, crowds in Afghanistan *and* Pakistan were chanting "Death to Obama!" in response to NATO military actions.

Nor were other anti-Americans appeased for very long. At the Copenhagen climate summit in December 2009, Venezuela's Hugo Chávez raged: "President Obama got the Nobel Peace Prize almost the same day as he sent 30,000 soldiers to kill innocent people in Afghanistan!"

A survey of international attitudes by World Public Opinion in July 2009 suggested that, while Barack Obama was personally popular with foreigners, attitudes to the United States had barely been impacted by his victory. The United States was still liked by her traditional friends, still loathed by her old foes. A majority of respondents in fifteen of the nineteen nations surveyed believed that the United States was coercing other states through superior force, and a majority in seventeen of the nineteen nations complained that the United States flouted international law.

There are certain positions that any U.S. president, if he is sensitive to public opinion and to congressional majorities, must take; and these tend to be the positions that make anti-Americans detest him. The fact that the facilities at Guantánamo are still open, for example, has prompted rage, not only in the Muslim world, but in Europe. Likewise, the refusal to publish photographs from Abu Ghraib. And, come to that, the fact that there still are American soldiers in Afghanistan.

"World's Hopes Dashed by George W. Obama," was the headline in the *Financial Times Deutschland* when the closure of Guantánamo was deferred. The Munich-based *Süddeutsche Zeitung*, in an editorial titled "Obama's Great Mistake," commented: "Obama's people certainly imagined things differently, but reality has caught up with them. . . . Bush light, so to speak: Obama is discrediting both himself and the United States."

To get a sense of what Europeans don't like about the United States, glance through some of the headlines that have appeared in *Der Spiegel* since Barack Obama's inauguration: "From Mania to Distrust: Europe's Obama Euphoria Wanes," "Torturing for America," "American Gays and Lesbians Feel Betrayed by Obama," "GM Insolvency Proves America's Global Power Is Waning," "American Recession Food: The Fat Crisis." (This last, if you're wondering, was all about how low-paid Americans had been driven by the downturn to subsist on McDonald's, which was making the country even more obese and diabetic.)

Here is the veteran British commentator John Pilger, writing in the *New Statesman* in December 2009:

> *Barack Obama is the leader of a contemporary Oceania [the American superpower in George Orwell's 1984]. In two speeches at the close of the decade, the Nobel Peace Prize–winner affirmed that peace was no longer peace, but rather a permanent war that "extends well beyond Afghanistan and Pakistan" to "disorderly regions, failed states, diffuse enemies." He called this "global security" and invited our gratitude. To the people of Afghanistan, which the United States has invaded and occupied, he said wittily: "We have no interest in occupying your country."*

Presidents come and go. But the fundamentals of U.S. foreign policy do not. The things that anti-Americans dislike cannot be expunged by executive decree.

Critics of the United States are not, as a rule, actuated by opposition to a particular policy or a particular administration. It is the entire package that they reject: free elections, small government, private property, open competition, inequality of outcome. They will not be appeased by the cap-and-trade rules, or by state health care, or by higher taxes, or by the abolition of the death penalty. Their hostility is existential.

This book is not aimed at convinced anti-Americans. It is aimed, rather, at those within the United States who have become blasé about their transcendent political inheritance. As Edmund Burke observed, constitutions that grow up over centuries can be torn down in weeks. The freedoms enjoyed by Americans today are the fruit of seeds transported across the Atlantic centuries ago and scattered in the rich humus of the New World. It is not accidental that the United States enjoys dispersed jurisdiction, limited government, strong local democracy, low taxes, and personal freedom. These things came about through design: the brilliant design of extraordinary men.

It follows that fundamentally altering that design will make America less American. This generation, like any generation, is entitled to opt for a different model: to embrace state intervention, higher taxes, federal czars, government regulation. But have no doubt about the consequences. Changing America into a different country will mean forsaking the most successful constitutional model in the world. It will mean abandoning the vision of your founders—a vision that has served to make your country rich and strong and free. It will mean betraying your ancestors and disinheriting your posterity. It is, in the narrowest and most literal sense, un-American. Before taking such a step, it is worth pausing to consider what you would lose.

2

AMERICAN DEMOCRACY WORKS

Kindly separated by nature and a wide ocean from the ex-
terminating havoc of one quarter of the globe; too high-
minded to endure the degradations of the others;
possessing a chosen country, with room enough for our
descendants to the thousandth and thousandth generation; entertaining a due sense of our equal right to the use
of our own faculties, to the acquisitions of our own industry, to honor and confidence from our fellow-citizens, resulting not from birth, but from our actions and their
sense of them—with all these blessings, what more is necessary to make us a happy and a prosperous people? Still
one thing more, fellow-citizens—a wise and frugal Government, which shall restrain men from injuring one another,
shall leave them otherwise free to regulate their own pur-
suits of industry and improvement, and shall not take
from the mouth of labor the bread it has earned.

—THOMAS JEFFERSON, 1800

A few months ago, I found myself addressing the Republican committee of a rural county in a southern
state. Its members looked much as I had expected members of the Republican committee of a rural county in a
southern state to look: rugged and sunburned. During

the question and answer session, I was asked why the GOP, having dominated late twentieth-century politics, was faring so badly.

I replied that, as far as I could see, one of the party's most serious mistakes had been its retreat from localism. The Republicans started winning in the 1960s when they embraced states' rights and the devolution of power. They started losing forty years later when they abandoned these principles. The audience growled its approval and so, perhaps incautiously, I began to list the areas where the Bush administration had wrongly extended central power, ranging from the rise in federal spending to the attempt to strike down state laws on same-sex unions. When I mentioned same-sex unions, a rustle went through the room, and I winced inwardly: This, I thought, was perhaps not the wisest example to have offered the Republican committee of a rural county in a southern state.

Sure enough, after I had finished, a man with a beard and a red baseball cap sauntered up to me.

"Son," he said, "Ah 'preciate you comin', an' Ah 'greed with most of wut you said. But Ah must disagree with your position on so-called homosexual marriage."

He paused to hitch his jeans up his great belly, looking into the middle distance.

"Far as Ah kin see, not bein' under any pressure to git married is one of the main advantages Ah enjoy as a gay man."

Truly, I thought, America is an extraordinary coun-

try. Every time you think you've got it sussed, it sur-
prises you. It is the sheer diversity of the United States
that makes anti-Americanism so perverse. All humanity
is represented in one nation, rendering the dislike of
that nation an act of misanthropy.

While researching this book, I experienced a measure
of that diversity. I visited California and Colorado, Florida and Georgia, New York and Pennsylvania, Washington, D.C., and Washington state. I met industrialists and
financiers, conservatives and liberals, town councilors
and state legislators, journalists and think-tankers. I spoke
to the most distinguished audience I expect ever to address: a closed meeting of the forty Republican senators.
At the end of it all, one conclusion towered over the rest:
Most Americans don't realize how lucky they are.

It is human nature to take familiar things for granted.
So let me, in this chapter, set out some of the things that
strike an outside observer about the U.S. political system.

The first observation is that, for all the grumbles
and the scornful jokes, most people have faith in the
system. This might seem a strange thing to say: Elected
representatives are the target of as many cynical re-
marks in the United States as elsewhere, and first-time
candidates often make a big deal out of not being politicians. One of my little girls has a book called *Vote for
Duck*, given to her by a kind American friend: Its con-
ceit is that a farmyard duck rises, first to run the farm,
then to become a governor, and finally to win the presi-

dency by repeatedly running under the slogan "Vote for a duck, not a politician!"

Behind the sarcasm, though, there is an underlying confidence. Think of the television series *The West Wing*. Its premise is that most politicians, including the ones you disagree with, are patriots who are doing their best. While it makes criticisms of Washington, its essential tone is laudatory. Even the right-wing Republicans who are presented least sympathetically, such as the John Goodman character who, in a bizarre twist, moves from being speaker of the House of Representatives to temporarily occupying the White House under the Twenty-fifth Amendment, are shown, when the chips are down, placing their country before their personal ambitions.

Believe me when I tell you that such a program is unimaginable—literally unimaginable—on my side of the Atlantic. British political dramas are invariably predicated on the idea that all elected representatives are petty, jobbing cowards. The most enjoyable such program was the late 1970s and early 1980s BBC production *Yes, Minister*, starring Nigel Hawthorne and Paul Eddington, which centered on a battle between a wily civil servant and the vote-grabbing politician who was notionally in charge of his department.

While the minister was shown as shallow and ambitious, there was a dash of warmth in the portrayal. Not so in later series. In *The New Statesman*, Rik Mayall played a selfish, greedy, perverted crook who rose swiftly through the ranks. In *House of Cards* Ian Richardson was a chief whip prepared to commit murder in order to become prime minister. In the current series *The Thick of It*, power is shown to have shifted definitively to the spin doctors, leaving the ministers as small-minded drones obsessed with their careers.

Things are even worse in Continental Europe. Canvassing in France and Spain, I have been left shaken by the way voters talk of their elected ministers. It is as though they are discussing agents of an occupying power. Latin America has been even more violently convulsed by an anti-politics mood: tinpot *caudillos* have taken power across the region, not because people expect them to do any good, but because they embody and articulate the rage that electorates felt against the old parties.

I'm not saying that U.S. politicians don't also come in for their share of mockery. But there is a difference between teasing people in authority—cutting them down to size—and fundamentally denying their legitimacy. Satirical shows in the United States strike most European viewers as so mild as to be deferential. The same is true of political interviews. While U.S. presenters can be searching and aggressive, you rarely catch them contorting their features into the knowing sneer that is the default expression of a European journalist interviewing a politician.

One might argue, of course, that this is merely a symptom of a wider cultural difference. The American media in general, with their editorial high-mindedness and determination to avoid bad language, are primmer than their British or European counterparts. Nonetheless, television can be a telling cultural marker, and fiction has always been a useful way to assess the temper of a civilization, to appraise its values and its preoccupations.

If you want something more empirical, though, look at the raw numbers. For a long time, it was axiomatic in Europe that low turnouts at American elections were a symptom of a corrupt plutocracy that was rigged against ordinary people. This view was based on a misreading of the figures. The U.S. political system is pluralist, in the sense that there are many more opportunities to vote than in most countries. One elector might care passionately about who her state senator is, but not care about the DA; her neighbor might have strong views on the composition of the school board, but be indifferent about the gubernatorial contest. In other words, while the turnout at any given election might be low, the number of people casting ballots at one time or another is significantly higher. The main role of the president is the direction of foreign and defense policy. It might be argued that, for voters who don't much care about international relations, the presidential election is less important than the more local polls.

More to the point, though, the premise of the Euro-sophists is wrong. Turnout at U.S. elections is rising. It is turnout at *European* elections that is falling. This is yet another instance of a phenomenon that we have already seen: the tendency of European critics of the United States to level accusations that not only are untrue, but apply more aptly to Europe than to America. It's an almost psycho-political phenomenon—a form of displacement.

Here are the figures:

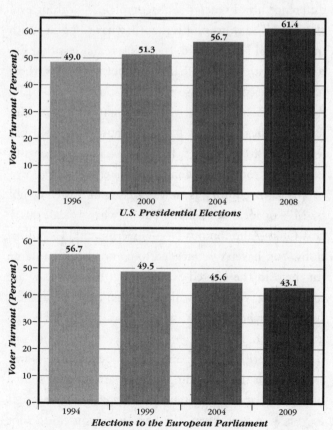

I have cited figures for the European Parliament because these constitute the only pan-continental polls, but the phenomenon of falling turnouts can also be observed within most of the EU member states. What is going on?

Anyone who has canvassed on the doorstep in Europe will tell you the answer. "It doesn't make any difference how I vote," people complain. "Nothing ever changes." The worst of it is that they have a point. With the best will in the world, there is less and less that European politicians *can* change. In recent decades, there has been a comprehensive shift in power in the EU: from elected representatives to permanent functionaries, from local councils to central bureaucracies, from legislatures to executives, from national parliaments to Eurocrats, from the citizen to the state.

My own country is now largely administered, not by MPs or local councilors, but by what we call quangos: Quasi-Autonomous Non-Governmental Organizations. You haven't yet needed to come up with a name for them in the United States but, at the rate they are multiplying, you soon will. A quango is a state agency, funded by the taxpayer, but at arm's length from the government.

Every British politician, if he is being honest, will tell you that these standing *apparats* are the true source of power in modern Britain. When a constituent writes to you with a problem, the best thing you can do for him, nine times out of ten, is to pass his complaint on to the appropriate bureaucracy: the Child Support Agency, the Highways Authority, the Learning and Skills Council, the Health and Safety Executive, the Food Standards Agency, the Equalities and Human Rights Commission.

As these functionariats have grown, representative government has shriveled. To quote the book for which this one is named, F. A. Hayek's *The Road to Serfdom*:

> *The delegation of particular technical tasks to separate bodies, while a regular feature, is yet the first step by which a democracy progressively relinquishes its powers.*

Of course, MPs don't like to advertise their power-lessness. They maintain the fiction that they are still in charge. As a result, voters tend to blame their politicians for the failings of a government machine that no longer answers to anyone. In the 1920s, Prime Minister Stanley Baldwin accused the press of exercising "Power without responsibility—the prerogative of the harlot throughout the ages." Today's MPs have the opposite: responsibility without power. Ceasing to be authoritative, they have become contemptible.

The extent to which voters despise their politicians was brutally exposed in 2009 by the Westminster expenses crisis. I won't bore you with full details of the scandal: This is, after all, a book about American, not

British, politics. To cut a long story short, a journalistic enquiry under a newly passed Freedom of Information Act required the House of Commons to publish details of every expense claim submitted by MPs. Some of the claims were outrageous. Most were not. The so-called Additional Costs Allowance had been set up to allow MPs from constituencies outside London to maintain a second home in the capital, and most of the receipts were for everyday household items: food, furniture, and so on.

Such was the mood of the country, though, that no one was especially minded to distinguish between the legitimate and the illegitimate claims. The MPs who had behaved scandalously—stretching the definition of their "main" residence, for example—were treated in exactly the same way as those who had behaved within the spirit and letter of the rules. The revelation that someone had claimed for a sofa or a frying pan was treated as an abominable scandal. Why? Because the affair wasn't really about expenses. It was about a much deeper-rooted sense that politicians had become parasitical. As long as MPs were unable to deliver meaningful improvements in their constituents' lives, *any* claim they submitted was resented, be it large or small, extravagant or modest.

Of course, the fact that there was such a fuss— the story dominated the front pages for six months— suggested that, in Britain at least, people felt that they ought to look up to the House of Commons. They were angry because they felt let down by an institution that, deep down, they wanted to respect. In most of Europe, voters are beyond that stage. My Continental colleagues in the European Parliament simply couldn't grasp what the fuss was about. A French friend made me explain it to him three times, and then remarked. "So: the money was for furniture, and the MPs spent it on furniture. *Et alors?*" An Italian MEP told me that, in his country, something didn't become a scandal unless it involved mafia links, briefcases full of banknotes, and, ideally, an assassination or two.

———————

Are American politicians more virtuous than their European counterparts? No. Is corruption unknown in Washington? No. The difference between the two systems has to do, not with the integrity of the practitioners, but with location of sovereignty.

America's Founding Fathers were determined, above all, to prevent the concentration of power. They knew firsthand where such concentration led, and had spent years fighting the consequences. As Thomas Jefferson put it:

> *I do verily believe that if the principle were to prevail of a common law being in force in the United States (which principle possesses the general government at once of all*

the powers of the state governments, and reduces us to a
single consolidated government), it would become the
most corrupt government on the earth.

The framers of the Constitution in general, and Jefferson's followers in particular, were determined to diffuse power, to constrain those in authority, to ensure that decision-makers could never stop looking over their shoulders at those they purported to represent. And, by and large, they succeeded.

American political institutions have developed according to what we might loosely call Jeffersonian principles: the belief that the concentration of power leads to malfeasance; that decisions should be taken as closely as possible to the people they affect; and that decision-makers, wherever practicable, should be answerable through the ballot box.

In consequence, contemporary Americans enjoy a series of unusual, sometimes unique, Jeffersonian institutions: states' rights, recall mechanisms, open primaries, referendum and initiative procedures, term limits, balanced budget rules, the direct election of public officials from the sheriff to the school board. If the U.S. Constitution was the genotype, these features of modern American democracy are the phenotype—the practices that have grown up according to the DNA encoded at Philadelphia.

It is, as I say, human nature to take for granted the

institutions that you have known throughout your life. Pause, then, to consider the difference between the United States and those nations that lack these political practices.

Take open primaries. Eleven years in public life have convinced me that open primaries are the strongest possible guarantee of a free and independent parliament. As long as they exist, no politician can afford to forget his electorate. Take them away, and you allow a government with a majority in the legislature to rule almost without constraint.

Again, let me compare the British and American dispensations (and again, as we shall see presently, things are worse in Continental Europe than in the United Kingdom). British election rules, unlike those prevalent across most of Europe, are similar to those in the United States. Both countries elect their legislators by first-past-the-post. Majoritarian voting is naturally conducive to a two-party system. In most of Europe, by contrast, there is proportional representation, which means that many more parties sit in the assembly, and that coalition government is the norm.

Although the rules are similar, the practice is very different. In Britain, as in the United States, most constituencies are "owned" by one of the two main parties. In four out of the past five British general elections, fewer than 9 percent of seats went from one party to the other. The exception was the Labour landslide of 1997, which brought Tony Blair to power. Even here, though, 73 percent of constituencies were retained by the parties that already held them.

In other words, 73 percent of British MPs need not worry about being voted out at election time. The only way they will lose their jobs is if their whips deny them the right to stand under their party colors.

Accordingly, instead of answering downward to their constituents, they answer upward to their party leaders. This skewing of incentives contributes to the creation of a separate political caste: a set of people whose values and preoccupations differ from those of the electors they notionally represent. On a whole series of issues, from tougher sentencing to supra-nationalism, voters are reconciled to being brushed aside by a *bien-pensant* elite.

Worse, the ease with which party leaders control their MPs means that Parliament has ceased to be a meaningful check on the executive. As long as one party commands a majority in the House of Commons, and as long as the careers of the MPs in that party depend on the goodwill of the whips, the administration is effectively unconstrained.

Americans might not realize how unusual they are in enjoying a genuine separation of powers—*de facto* as well as *de jure*. When Barack Obama proposed his stimulus package, every line of the budget was debated and haggled over by elected representatives who knew that, within a couple of years, they would have to explain themselves to their voters, who are also taxpayers. In the United Kingdom, by contrast, Gordon Brown decreed a much larger package in *per capita* terms, without so much as summoning Parliament.

In the seventeenth century, Englishmen fought a civil war to establish the principle that only the House of Commons might raise revenue through taxation for the national government. Yet so overbearing is the modern executive, so feeble its invigilators, that a twenty-first-century prime minister enjoys powers beyond the dreams of the Stuart kings.

In most European countries, where legislators are elected on party lists through proportional representation, politicians are even further removed from their electorates. If you are near the top of your party list, you are effectively irremovable. So, naturally enough, you spend your time sucking up to the person who determines which position on that list you will occupy: your party leader. Once you have secured a high-ranking place, you are invulnerable to public opinion. Even if your party suffers a heavy defeat, you will still be in the national assembly and with a fair chance of being in government as a minor coalition partner.

A rarely remarked but malign consequence of proportional representation is that most of the parties are in power most of the time. They therefore have no incentive to reduce the powers of the state—or, come to that, the perks of the politicians who are employed by it.

In Britain and the United States, parties alternate in power. The party in opposition generally seeks to constrain the government; and the majority party, knowing that it will one day be in opposition, tends to be circumspect about building a machine that will eventually fall into the hands of its opponents. A two-party pendulum, in other words, tends to keep the state smaller, and the citizen commensurately bigger.

In countries where some parties are more or less permanently in office, these constraints do not apply. One way to measure the impact is to compare the share of GDP taken by the state. In the United States, over the past three decades, the percentage has tended to be in the high thirties; in Britain, in the low forties; in European countries with coalition governments, in the high forties.

Open primaries don't just serve to strengthen the legislature vis-à-vis the executive. They also ensure that political parties are rooted in public opinion. I visited Georgia in 2009—a state which, astonishingly, had never had a Republican governor before the current incumbent, Sonny Perdue. While I was there, a state legislator kindly invited me to join him for a day's hunting. As he outlined his philosophy, his gun over his arm, I found

myself marveling at the consequences of open primaries. The congressman described himself as a conservative Democrat. When I had previously encountered
that phrase in the U.S. media, it often carried connota-
tions of "southern racist," but this man was in no way
nostalgic for the old South, and was well aware that he
owed his majority to African American voters. He was
a thoroughly modern American who happened to believe in patriotism, localism, low taxes, and personal
freedom. When I asked him what had made him join
the same party as Ted Kennedy, he replied simply:
"Mine is a Democratic district; my voters are Democrats." The real election, for him, had been the primary,
in which he had defeated nine other candidates.

How extraordinary, I thought, to have a system
where politicians see their role as being to represent
their constituencies in their parties rather than the
other way around; where policy is made bottom-up
rather than top-down. My own electoral division, South
East England, is, like Georgia, a pretty right-wing
place—certainly in the sense of being fiscally conservative. But, whereas both parties in Georgia try to reflect
the temper of the local populace, Labour candidates in
South East England are, if anything, further to the left
than in the rest of the country, reflecting as they do the
prejudices of tiny selection committees.

Open primaries, in other words, don't just guarantee a purer form of democracy; they also ensure greater

diversity within the legislature. They are perhaps the single most effective way to ensure that the government is accountable to the governed. Yet they are almost wholly unknown outside the United States.

Unknown, at least, for the present. Within the past year, the British Conservatives have selected three parliamentary candidates through open primaries—an innovation that is likely to spread for the simple reason that, in a contest between a candidate imposed by a local party committee and one chosen by the wider electorate, the latter will almost always win. When one party adopts open primaries, the others will have to follow if they want to remain in business. Once this happens, all the parties will be held within the gravitational pull of public opinion, varying in their orbits, but unable wholly to cast off the surly bonds of Earth.

If open primaries serve to make political parties accountable, the direct election of officials performs the same function for the administrative machine as a whole. Again, Americans might not be aware of how exceptionally fortunate they are in being able to elect their sheriffs, district attorneys, school boards, and all the rest. It is worth taking a moment to ponder why this matters.

A functioning modern democracy ought to ensure that civil servants work for the rest of the population. In the private sector, firms are accountable through the market. In the public sector, state officials are meant to be accountable through the ballot box. If they are not so accountable, human nature being what it is, they eventually will start to suit themselves.

I don't mean that they will be lazy (although, by the law of averages, some of them will be). Rather, I mean that they will discharge their duties according to the criteria favored by their colleagues and the experts within their own fields rather than the broader public. Teachers will start applying fancy educational theories that fly in the face of common sense. Police officers will start pursuing soft targets in preference to dangerous criminals. Judges will be reluctant to incarcerate malefactors.

To put it another way, the default setting of the public sector, in any country, tends to be well to the left of the population at large. This is perhaps no surprise: Those whose livelihoods depend on the taxpayer are bound to see things slightly differently from those who operate in the private sector. But in the United States, unlike in most places, the direct election of those in charge of local services drags officials back into the mainstream, forcing them to follow local people's priorities instead of their own. To see what would happen without this discipline, look at countries where there are no such elections.

Let me give one example. Outside the United States, it is very unusual to have any mechanisms of direct democratic control over the police. In Britain, the notional regulation of constabularies comes from bodies known as Police Authorities, on which local councilors sit alongside a number of co-opted nominees. These bodies are almost wholly unknown to the wider public and have come, over the years, to see it as their role to champion "their" chief constables.

The result? British police chiefs have drifted further and further away from public opinion. Ask them what their priorities are, and they will talk about cracking down on sexist language in the canteen, recruiting more ethnic minority officers, improving their relations with the gay community. While none of these objectives is intrinsically wrong, it is hard to avoid the conclusion that they have displaced, rather than complemented, what ought to be the core task of the police: being beastly to scoundrels.

Consider the case of Sir Ian Blair, until 2008 the head of London's Metropolitan Police, and thus the United Kingdom's most senior police officer. Early in his career, it became clear that Sir Ian saw the promotion of multiculturalism as the chief function of a police force. When two young girls were murdered by a sex offender, he chided the press for giving more column inches to their case than to black crime victims (inaccurately as well as insensitively, as a survey of column inches revealed). As street crime rose in London, he managed to find the money to hire fourteen diversity advisers. He spent millions of pounds redesigning the logo of the Metropolitan Police to make it more "accessible." At the same time, he was careful to cozy up to the Labour government, lobbying openly in favor of its Draconian proposals to intern suspects for six weeks without charge.

Unsurprisingly, Londoners concluded that their vain, hypersensitive, publicity-obsessed police chief was taking his eye off what ought to have been his main job. Matters came to a head in July 2005 when, in the aftermath of a terrorist attack on the London Underground, anti-terrorist officers shot dead a Brazilian electrician in the belief that he had been one of the bombers. At first, the police refused to admit their error, and Sir Ian announced that a man had been shot as part of a security operation. When it became clear that an innocent victim had been killed, the police started spreading false rumors in an attempt to exculpate themselves: It was said that the man had been an illegal immigrant, that he had jumped the barrier and attempted to flee.

Eventually, public pressure mounted to the extent that, following a damning inquiry, the London Assembly passed a motion of no confidence in the hapless chief constable in November 2007. Not that he cared. On the contrary, knowing that he was invulnerable to democratic control, Sir Ian taunted the assemblymen with their powerlessness, declaring: "I have stated my position. If you have the power to remove me, go on."

Twelve months later, Sir Ian negotiated a generous redundancy package, which left him with virtually the same income as if he had served out his term. Only then did he volunteer to step down.

I don't want to pick on Sir Ian Blair. He is an inevitable by-product of a system in which there is no mechanism to align the priorities of public servants with those of the public they notionally serve. It is worth noting, though, that unaccountable public sector executives—quangocrats, in the British vernacular—fight very hard to avoid being made answerable. When the Labour Party brought forward modest proposals to strengthen the democratic component of the Police Authorities, a massive lobbying campaign was waged against it by police chiefs. When the Conservatives announced that they would go further and adopt a U.S. system of directly elected sheriffs, mass resignations were threatened.

Democracy is more easily truncated than extended. Attempts to introduce the direct election of public officials on the U.S. model invariably trigger a massive resistance campaign from the unelected beneficiaries of the current system. But the reverse is not true. Governments can set up new agencies and committees—or new federal czars—with little protest. Which is why Americans shouldn't be complacent. Once power shifts from elected representatives to appointed officials, it is no simple matter to shift it back.

Open primaries and direct elections are the chief guarantors of modern Jeffersonian democracy. But other defensive ramparts have been thrown up alongside them. These vary from place to place: Some states favor term limits, others recall procedures; some limit how many days their legislatures can meet, others allow for ballots by popular initiative. Indeed, there is something intrinsically Jeffersonian in the fact that each state is free to design its own political institutions. As we shall see in the next chapter, the advantage of pluralism—the freedom to trial new ideas, and to copy what works elsewhere—is itself a bulwark against overweening government.

Taken collectively, these procedures not only tilt the balance from the state to the citizen; they also give purpose and meaning to the act of voting. They encourage the phenomenon of the citizen legislator. They explain the culture of optimism that produced *The West Wing* rather than *Yes, Minister.* They contextualize something that strikes almost every foreign observer about U.S. politics: the absence of cynicism. (Euro-sophists call it "naïveté" which, when you think about it, means the same thing.)

Americans sometimes put the difference down to culture. The United States, they say, is naturally more optimistic than the Old World, with its deference, its class systems, its monarchies, and so on. But this explanation won't do. Culture is not a numinous entity that exists alongside institutions; it is a product of those institutions. The reason Americans are relatively optimistic about their democracy is that they have been habituated from an early age to the idea that their ballots can effect meaningful change.

Forty million people worldwide watched Barack Obama's inauguration: an extraordinary affirmation of faith in the U.S. system. Can you imagine a similar number of people tuning in to watch the results of elections to the Russian Duma, or the annual meeting of the National People's Congress in Beijing, or the nomination hearings for European Commissioners? To gauge the success of the American dispensation, contrast it to the alternatives.

3

1787 VERSUS 2004:
A TALE OF TWO
UNIONS

O ye that love mankind! Ye that dare oppose, not only the
tyranny, but the tyrant, stand forth! Every spot of the old
world is overrun with oppression. Freedom hath been
hunted round the globe. Asia, and Africa, have long expelled her. Europe regards her like a stranger, and England hath given her warning to depart. O! receive the
fugitive, and prepare in time an asylum for mankind.

—TOM PAINE, 1775

On my desk before me as I write are two constitutions:
that of the United States and that of the EU. To demonstrate what makes the United States exceptional, I
can do no better than to compare the two texts.

The U.S. Constitution, with all its amendments, is
7,200 words long. The EU Constitution, now formally
known as the Lisbon Treaty, is 76,000.

The U.S. Constitution concerns itself with broad
principles, such as the balance between state and federal authorities. The EU Constitution busies itself with

such details as space exploration, the rights of disabled people, and the status of asylum seekers.

The U.S. Constitution, in particular the Bill of Rights, is mainly about the liberty of the individual. The EU Constitution is mainly about the power of the state.

The U.S. Declaration of Independence, which foreshadowed the constitutional settlement, promises "life, liberty and the pursuit of happiness." The EU's equivalent, the Charter of Fundamental Rights and Freedoms, guarantees its citizens the right to strike action, free health care, and affordable housing.

If you think I'm being unreasonable in comparing the two constitutions, incidentally, let me refer you to the chief author of the European Constitution, the former French president Valéry Giscard d'Estaing. At the opening session of the drafting convention in 2002, he told delegates: "This is Europe's Philadelphia moment," and went on to compare himself to Thomas Jefferson—inaccurately as well as immodestly, since Jefferson wasn't present when the U.S. Constitution was drafted; he was, as Giscard d'Estaing might have been expected to be aware, the U.S. ambassador to Paris.

To see quite how preposterous Giscard's comparison was, consider the way in which the two constitutions were adopted. The U.S. Constitution came into effect only following ratification by specially convened assemblies in eleven of the member states, with the remaining two, North Carolina and Rhode Island, falling into line soon afterward. Initially, the authors of the EU Constitution had intended to use the modern equivalent: referendums. It soon became clear, however, that the referendums might produce unwelcome results. In 2005, the document was put to the vote in two of the EU's founding states, France and the Netherlands. Both rejected it: by 54 percent and 62 percent respectively.

At this stage, one might have expected the leaders of the EU to take the old text off the table and try to come up with one more acceptable to public opinion. But that's not how things work in Brussels. Public opinion is treated as an obstacle to overcome, not a reason to change direction. Realizing that their proposals for deeper integration were likely to be rejected at the ballot box, the heads of government resolved not to allow any more votes. The text of the European Constitution was scrambled. A team of lawyers, as Giscard cheerfully admitted, went through the document line by line, keeping the effects identical, but rendering the articles "unreadable." The new version was rebaptized as the Lisbon Treaty, and the national governments solemnly announced that their previous promise of a referendum no longer applied.

There was one exception. The national constitution of Ireland requires referendums to be held on any proposal that would substantially alter the location of power. Although the Irish government dearly would have liked to avoid a popular vote, it couldn't, since the European Constitution, or Lisbon Treaty, plainly amounted to a substantial shift of power from Dublin to Brussels. Accordingly, on June 12, 2008, Ireland voted on the text. Once again, it was rejected. And, once again, the EU brushed aside the rejection and pushed ahead regardless.

In the run-up to polling day, the President of the European Commission, José Manuel Durrão Barroso, had declared: "There is no Plan B." Many Irish voters innocently took this to mean that, if they voted no, the text would be withdrawn. But what Barroso actually meant was that Plan A would be resubmitted over and over again. Extraordinary pressure was put on Ireland, and the country was threatened with isolation and bankruptcy. At the same time, a massive EU-funded propaganda campaign was launched. On October 2, 2009, demoralized by the effects of the financial crisis, which had been more serious in Ireland than anywhere else in the EU, Irish voters caved in and, in a second referendum, reversed their verdict.

Bertolt Brecht's words apply eerily to the ratification of the European Constitution and, indeed, to the story of European integration more broadly: "Wouldn't it therefore be easier to dissolve the people, and elect another in their place?"

Giscard's Jeffersonian pretensions are rendered risible by the Eurocrats' contempt for the masses. Where the U.S. Constitution represented a popular impulse toward a new form of government, the EU Constitution was imposed on visibly unenthusiastic electorates. Where the one was based on empowering the people and controlling the state, the other was based on empowering the state and controlling the people.

Indeed, the difference between the American and European unions can be inferred from the opening words of their foundational texts. The U.S. Constitution begins, "We, the People . . ." The EU Constitution, in the form of the amended European Treaties, begins, "His Majesty the King of the Belgians . . ."

As we saw in the preceding chapter, states tend to develop according to the DNA encoded at their conception. The United States was fortunate in the timing and circumstances of its birth. The late eighteenth century was perhaps the moment in the development of Western philosophy, or at least British political thought, when there was maximum emphasis on the freedom of the citizen. Because the new republic was born out of a popular revolt against a remote and autocratic government, its founders were determined to prevent a recurrence of the abuses against which they had taken up arms.

Their preoccupations are plainly visible, both in the debates that accompanied the drafting of the U.S. Constitution, and in the resulting text. They wanted to be certain that laws could not be passed without consent, nor taxes levied except by the will of elected representatives. They wanted the president to be controlled by Congress, and knew what they were doing when they placed the legislature in Article One and the executive in Article Two. They wanted the individual to be protected against arbitrary government or punitive levies. They wanted jurisdiction to be dispersed, with the federal authorities exercising limited and contingent functions while residual authority was vested in the states.

By and large, they succeeded. There have been alterations to the system they planned. The twentieth century saw the White House grow at the expense of Congress, and the federal government at the expense of the states—both, as we shall see, with unhappy consequences. But, relative to other countries, the United States has retained a remarkably devolved and democratic form of government. The Constitution did precisely what it was designed to do, limiting the growth of central power and encouraging the development of a pluralist polity. All the peculiar features of American democracy that we discussed in the preceding chapter—referendums, recall votes, term limits, open primaries, dispersed jurisdiction, direct elections—are the result of the exalted doctrines that were committed to paper at the old courthouse in Philadelphia in 1787.

Unfortunately, the EU is also a child of its time. Its Founding Fathers, no less than Washington or Madison, designed institutions to prevent a recurrence of the troubles through which they had recently passed. They had come through the terrible experience of World War II, and were determined to prevent future conflicts at any price. This they hoped to achieve by pooling, first the economic resources, and then the administrative structures, of Europe's nations, so that wars between them should become logistically impossible. The objective of political integration was seen as overriding: more important than either personal freedom or democratic accountability.

Most of the framers of the U.S. Constitution had been involved in a rising against an undemocratic regime, and consequently saw representative government as a defense against tyranny. But the experience of the Euro-patriarchs, above all Jean Monnet and Robert Schuman, had been very different. They recoiled with horror from the memory of the plebiscitary democracy that had preceded World War II. They fretted that, left to themselves, voters might fall prey to unscrupulous demagogues. Accordingly, they were determined to constrain the ballot box and moderate the will of the people.

The system they designed vested supreme power in the hands of an appointed European Commission. Not only is the Commission the EU's executive, equivalent to the White House; it also has a monopoly of the right to initiate legislation. This extraordinary and outrageous concentration of power is rarely remarked upon, possibly because it has become familiar through time. But it is worth contemplating the paradox that the twenty-seven members of the EU, all of them democratic in themselves, have submitted themselves collectively to a system of government in which supreme power is wielded by appointed officials who have been deliberately made invulnerable to the ballot box.

When the EU swats aside inconvenient referendum results, it isn't behaving perversely. It is faithfully obeying the creed of its founders, who believed that public opinion often needed to be tempered by a class of sober functionaries. After all, had the EU been democratic, and had each successive transfer of power from the nations to Brussels been referred to the voters for permission, the project never would have taken off.

Which brings us to another critical difference between the two federations. In America, there was a sense of common nationhood prior to the formal federation of the old colonies. Most of the characteristics that define nationality—a similar culture, compatible religious practices, comparable historical experience and, above all, a common language—already existed in America, and it is striking that, when the Constitution was being negotiated, the word "nation" was generally applied to America as a whole (although the word "country" was more often used for a particular state). Although there was a strong and laudable tradition of localism, there was also a tangible American *demos*: a community with which Americans identified when they used the word "we."

Almost no one in Europe feels a comparable sense of pan-Continental affinity. There is no European public opinion; there are no European media. Although the EU provides lavish funds to incentivize the creation of cross-border political parties, politics are played out entirely on a national basis. There is, in short, no European *demos*. If you take the *demos* out of democracy, you are left only with the *kratos*: the power of a system that must compel by force of law what it cannot ask in the name of civic patriotism.

The paradox is that, in pursuing political integration without the consent of their peoples, the leaders of the EU are turning their backs on Europe's heritage. The richness of European civilization has always resided in its diversity, its pluralism, its variety. Yet, comparing the political structures of the United States and the EU, we see that those values, exported across the Atlantic centuries ago, are thriving better in their new home than on their native soil. Rather as several varieties of European grape survived in California when the nineteenth-century phylloxera blight wiped out the ancestral vines in Europe, so the political structures that brought Europe to global hegemony are better preserved in North America than in the Old World.

What was it, after all, that made Western civilization the dominant force of the past five hundred years? Europe started with few advantages. Compared to the great Oriental civilizations—the Ming, Mogul, and Ottoman monarchies—the squabbling nations at the western tip of the Eurasian landmass seemed to have little going for them. Technologically, they were nowhere near as advanced as the great Asian empires, which far surpassed Europe in their knowledge of astronomy and mathematics, of cartography and medicine, of canals and gunpowder, of paper money.

Why, then, did Europe become the hegemonic power of the modern age? Why didn't the Chinese, as one might have expected, sail round the Cape to discover Portugal? The most convincing answer was offered by the Australian historian E. L. Jones in his 1981 book *The European Miracle*—although Jones's hypothesis was later carried to a much wider audience in Paul Kennedy's *The Rise and Fall of the Great Powers*.

To condense an elaborate and subtle dissertation, Jones argued that Europe's success resided in the fact that it never became a unified state, but rather remained a states system. Where the Oriental empires became centralized, bureaucratized, and heavily taxed, Europe's princedoms were constantly competing one with another. New ideas were trialed in one country and, if successful, copied by others. The lack of a strong central authority encouraged a culture of

enterprise and adventure, of exploration and mercan-
tilism.

It tended also to encourage political freedom. Many
European advances were driven by the phenomenon of
the refugee. As long as there was somewhere to flee to,
the power of the autocrat was checked. As long as there
were competing states, no dictatorship would be secure.
As Edward Gibbon put it in his masterpiece, *The Decline
and Fall of the Roman Empire*:

> *The division of Europe into a number of independent
> states, connected, however, with each other by the gen-
> eral resemblance of religion, language, and manners, is
> productive of the most beneficial consequences to the lib-
> erty of mankind. A modern tyrant, who should find no
> resistance either in his own breast, or in his people,
> would soon experience a gentle restraint from the exam-
> ple of his equals, the dread of present censure, the advice
> of his allies, and the apprehension of his enemies. The
> object of his displeasure, escaping from the narrow limits
> of his dominions, would easily obtain, in a happier cli-
> mate, a secure refuge, a new fortune adequate to his
> merit, the freedom of complaint, and perhaps the means
> of revenge.*

This observation was already demonstrably true in
Gibbon's time. Britain's ascendancy over France began
when, with the Revocation of the Edict of Nantes, the

Bourbons expelled their Protestant subjects, thereby driving some of their most enterprising and inventive people to settle in competitor states. It was to be vindicated again in the story of the defeats of Bonapartism, Nazism, and the Soviet tyranny.

Which is why it is so tragic to see Europe abandoning the pluralism that was its greatest strength, and instead pursuing the Ming-Mogul-Ottoman road toward uniformity, mandarinism, and central control. Most EU member states are coy about admitting what percentage of their national legislation comes from Brussels. In Germany, however, a thorough analysis was produced by the Federal Justice Ministry in answer to a parliamentary question. It concluded that an extraordinary 84 percent of all the laws in Germany were there to give effect to EU directives or regulations. Unless and until other governments supply their own figures, it seems not unreasonable to assume that that figure would not vary much around the EU. If that figure is even remotely accurate, a European superstate is already upon us.

Quite apart from the negative impact on democratic accountability, this centralization of power has deleterious consequences for economic prosperity. As the Nobel Laureate Gary Becker has written:

> *Competition among nations tends to produce a race to the top rather than to the bottom by limiting the ability of powerful and voracious groups and politicians in each*

*nation to impose their will at the expense of the interests
of the vast majority of their populations.*

It's a phenomenon that political scientists call "systems
competition." The United States is a fine example of its
beneficial effects—although less and less so as the federal
government expands. The EU is a depressing example of
what the United States might turn into: a federation that is
prepared to sacrifice prosperity for the sake of uniformity.

External competition is perhaps the major constraint upon a *dirigiste* government. A state can raise
taxes only up to a certain point before capital begins to
flow into overseas jurisdictions. It can offer its workers
generous social entitlements only up to a certain point
before entrepreneurs, firms, and eventually whole industries start to relocate to more attractive regimes.

As Milton Friedman put it:

*Competition among national governments in the public
services they provide and in the taxes they impose is
every bit as productive as competition among individuals or enterprises in the goods and services they offer for
sale and the prices at which they offer them.*

Of course, many of the supporters of European integration have an ideological dislike of competition.
There were few economic liberals among the EU's early
leaders. Some of the Euro-patriarchs were socialists.

Most were Christian Democrats, heirs to the corporatist and centrist political tradition that had begun in the late nineteenth century as an attempt to lure Catholic working men away from Marxism. For many Eurointegrationists, much of the appeal of the project lies in the fact that it is an alternative to the "jungle capitalism" that supposedly defines the United States.

The first generation of Eurocrats believed that supra-nationalism would remove the competitive restraints on governments. Instead of the difficult political task of persuading their electorates to accept spending cuts or less generous entitlements, EU governments could simply export their costs to their neighbors. They believed, too, that big was beautiful: that the advantages of a large home market would outweigh the costs of reduced competition.

Setting aside the ideological objections to this vision, it has become technologically obsolescent. In the 1950s, regional blocs were a much more credible proposition than they are today, when the Internet has eliminated distance, and when capital can surge around the globe at the touch of a button. It is no longer possible to ignore competition from the other side of the world. Competition from China and India is every bit as real as competition from Slovakia or Greece.

We can see, moreover, that the size of an economy is no guarantor of its success. If big really was beautiful, China would be more prosperous than Hong

Kong, Indonesia than Brunei, France than Monaco, the EU than Switzerland.

In fact, the reverse is true. There is an inverse correlation between size and prosperity. The wealthiest people in the world tend to live in very small states, as can be seen in this league table.

	STATE	INCOME PER CAPITA (U.S. DOLLARS, 2008)
1.	Liechtenstein	145,700
2.	Qatar	124,000
3.	Luxembourg	113,100
4.	Norway	98,200
5.	Ireland	65,800
6.	Switzerland	65,000
7.	Denmark	62,500
8.	Kuwait	60,900
9.	Iceland	57,700
10.	United Arab Emirates	56,300
11.	Jersey	56,200
12.	Sweden	53,600
13.	Finland	52,200
14.	Netherlands	52,200
15.	Austria	50,600
16.	Belgium	48,700
17.	Australia	48,100
18.	United States	46,900
19.	Canada	45,500
20.	France	44,700

Source: *CIA World Factbook*

As you will see, the list is dominated by micro-states. The only country in the top ten with a population of more than six million in Switzerland: a highly diffuse confederation.

You might be tempted to dismiss some of these territories as tax havens, but this is to beg the question. They became tax havens in the first place by having low taxes. And why did they have low taxes? Because they were able to avoid the waste and excess that plague larger territories.

It is enormously significant that the first large state on the list should be the United States: the big exception, in both senses. The reason the United States has done better than other macro-states is that, until now, it has governed itself like a confederation of statelets, allowing substantial autonomy to its constituent parts, and thereby retaining the chief advantages of small statehood: efficiency, lack of duplication, proximity to the electorate, limited bureaucracy.

Euro-integrationists dimly grasp that the assumptions of the 1950s no longer pertain, and that the EU is threatened by competition from more efficient polities. But their response is not to free up their own markets. Rather, it is to seek to globalize their costs, to extend Europe's socioeconomic model to other continents. The EU has poured resources into encouraging the development of regional blocs around the world: Mercosur, ASEAN, the Andean Community, the African, Caribbean, and Pacific Group of States. And it is investing its political capital in schemes designed to create a degree of global harmonization, such as the G20 and the Rio-Kyoto-Copenhagen process.

In November 2009, the EU appointed its first president: the former Belgian prime minister Herman Van Rompuy. At his very first press conference, Van Rompuy announced that he wanted the EU to return to "the economic and social agenda." Referring to the G20 Conference, he hailed 2009 as "the first year of global governance," and went on to describe the Copenhagen Climate Summit as "another step toward the global management of our planet."

Until now, the main obstacle to such global governance has come from Washington. Leaders of the EU, true to their founders' vision, have tended to favor supra-nationalism, believing that global technocracies are a surer form of government than vote-grabbing national politicians. Leaders of the United States, true likewise to *their* founders' vision, have supported national sovereignty, democratic accountability, and the dispersal of power.

Recently, though, things have started to change. The United States has been readier to accept a measure of supra-nationalism, and Barack Obama has indicated a willingness to share sovereignty on issues ranging from climate change to collaboration with the International Criminal Court. This international change in outlook has accompanied a change in the domestic arrangements of the United States: a shift toward greater central control and higher federal spending. America, in short, is becoming more European.

4

THE RETREAT FROM FEDERALISM

The powers delegated by the proposed Constitution to the federal government are few and defined. Those which are to remain in the State governments are numerous and indefinite. The former will be exercised principally on external objects, as war, peace, negotiation, and foreign commerce; with which last the power of taxation will, for the most part, be connected. The powers reserved to the several States will extend to all the objects which, in the ordinary course of affairs, concern the lives, liberties, and properties of the people, and the internal order, improvement, and prosperity of the State.

–JAMES MADISON, 1787

The Founding Fathers were in no doubt about the merits of decentralization. The autonomy of the individual states was, for them, "an auxiliary precaution," alongside representative democracy and the separation of powers, to prevent the growth of an overbearing government.

The dispersal of power has several other advantages, too. It stimulates competition and economic growth. It encourages experimentation and the spread of best practice. It brings government nearer to the people and, in doing so, makes it smaller and less wasteful. All these boons, however, are, so to speak, fringe benefits. U.S. federalism was chiefly designed to prevent the growth of a dictatorial central state.

As Thomas Jefferson put it in a private letter in 1812:

✓ *Our country is too large to have all its affairs directed by a single government. Public servants, at such a distance, and from under the eye of their constituents, must, from the circumstance of distance, be unable to administer and overlook all the details necessary for the good government of the citizens; and the same circumstance, by rendering detection impossible to their constituents, will invite the public agents to corruption, plunder, and waste.*

Don't make the mistake of thinking that these arguments belong in the pages of a history book. If anything, the framers were hundreds of years ahead of their time in anticipating modern public choice theory. They intuited something that political scientists were later able to study empirically. They understood that large administrations would become prey to vested interests, and that the law of dispersed costs and concentrated gains would make big government expensive, inefficient, and nepotistic. In the words of John McGinnis of Northwestern University Law School:

> *A large diverse democracy, where interest groups are held* ✓
> *in check by jurisdictional competition, substantially re-*
> *duces the incentives for individuals to seek rents through*
> *government action. Individuals will instead spend their*
> *time, on balance, in relatively more productive and*
> *peaceful activity.*

The founders, and the Jeffersonians in particular, were also ahead of their time in understanding that, in any state, there will always be a centripetal force exercised by the federal authorities. Again, they sensed by instinct a phenomenon that a later generation of political scientists was to identify and label. Professor Roland Vaubel of Mannheim University has carried out a major study of twenty-two federations, and found that, in all but one of them, there has been a tendency, over time, for power to shift from state or provincial authorities to the central government. He has identified a number of factors that drive the process of centralization. Provincial governments, for example, often refer a decision upward in order to overcome local opposition to a specific measure, which jurisdiction, once transferred, is ✓ almost never returned. Constitutions are usually interpreted by a supreme court whose members, being appointed at the federal level, tend to have a federal outlook. Powers delegated to the center in times of war or crisis are rarely devolved when the emergency passes.

Among the twenty-two nations surveyed, the only exception was Canada where, until the mid-1980s, the body equivalent to a supreme court was the British Privy Council, which, not being a Canadian institution, had no interest in strengthening the national authorities at the expense of the provinces. Everywhere else, many more powers were transferred upward than downward.

It is a measure of their genius that the Founding Fathers did their best to take precautions against this tendency, even though they had no direct experience of it. The Bill of Rights that they tacked on to the Constitution, in the form of the first ten Amendments, asserted the prerogatives of the citizen against national institutions, and at the same time protected the sovereignty of the states. The Tenth Amendment (originally proposed by Madison as the ninth) makes explicit what is implicit in the tone of the entire constitutional settlement:

The powers not delegated to the United States by the Constitution, nor prohibited by it to the States, are reserved to the States respectively, or to the people.

There were, inevitably, fierce arguments about where to draw the line between state sovereignty and federal authority: arguments that led, in time, to the Nullification Crisis and eventually to the Civil War. But what strikes the observer at this distance in time is how successful the authors of the Constitution were in securing their objectives. Even today, U.S. states in many ways enjoy more autonomy than whole nations within the European Union: They are able to set their own rates of indirect taxation, for example, and can decide whether or not to apply the death penalty.

That said, the United States has not been immune to the centralizing tendencies that have afflicted other federations. The twentieth century saw a transfer of powers from state to federal authorities, which resulted in a much larger and more unwieldy Washington administration.

The first shift in power happened under Theodore Roosevelt who, pleading the contingency of an active foreign policy, seized for the White House powers that had until then resided with Congress and the states. It was he who began to make widespread use of executive decrees as an instrument of administration. Indeed, the baleful statism of the second Roosevelt would not have been possible without the precedents established by the first.

To be fair, both Roosevelts were men of their time, as was Woodrow Wilson. During the first half of the twentieth century, most clever and fashionable people believed in the power of the state and the importance of government planning. The U.S. Congress was not immune to global currents of thought, and began to regulate whole industries that had previously operated with minimal oversight: railroads, food production, meat-packing, pharmaceuticals.

The founders had enshrined states' rights in the Constitution, and amending the Constitution was no simple matter. However, with confidence in federal institutions at its high-water mark, politicians were able to effect considerable transfers of power from state legislatures to Washington, bending the Constitution to their will. Indeed, the neatest way to measure the centralization of this era is by scanning the text of the sudden clutch of amendments.

There had been no amendments for forty-three years following Reconstruction. The Sixteenth Amendment, passed in 1913, was the first of a new set of measures aimed at strengthening the national government. It established the right of Congress to levy income tax, and did so in such broad and general language as would have horrified Jefferson:

> *The Congress shall have power to lay and collect taxes on incomes, from whatever source derived, without apportionment among the several States, and without regard to any census or enumeration.*

That amendment, as much as any other, revolution-ized the relationship between federal and state authori-ties. It gave Washington a massive financial advantage, and allowed Congress to make conditional grants to states in return for their discharge of particular policies. From then on, states often found themselves acting simply as the local administrators of a national policy—which was, of course, precisely the intention of the Wilson administration.

In the same year, the Seventeenth Amendment re-placed the old Senate, whose members had been nomi-nated by their state governments, with a directly elected chamber. While the change unquestionably reflected the mood of the times—the old system had given rise to some notorious cases of favoritism and corruption—it also fundamentally altered the federal character of the United States. From then on, the legislature was a wholly national institution, and the conception of the Senate as a guarantor of states' rights was, if not wholly eliminated, much weakened.

The Eighteenth Amendment, ratified in 1919, estab-lished Prohibition. It is a sign of the mood of those times that the sale and consumption of intoxicating liquors could ever have been seen as a proper field for federal reg-ulation. The Eighteenth Amendment, the only one ever to have been repealed, was perhaps the most egregious exam-ple of the appetite of national politicians to micromanage matters that can be administered locally perfectly well.

Finally, the Nineteenth Amendment, adopted in 1920, extended to the vote to women, a less contentious measure than its immediate predecessors, and one that followed the precedent of the Reconstruction amendments that extended the franchise to former slaves, but nonetheless one that reflected the federal government's belief that it had the power, not simply to define who was eligible to participate in nationwide ballots, but also to lay down how states must run their internal elections.

The centralization of the Wilson years was a prelude to the massive power grab of the New Deal. I know that, for many people, Franklin D. Roosevelt is a hero. And, as a British Conservative, I don't want to be churlish about the president who came to Churchill's aid when our need was greatest. But it is worth looking at his initiatives coldly, not least because of their relevance to our current era.

Most disastrous policies have been introduced at times of emergency. FDR, like Barack Obama, was elected during what looked like a crisis of capitalism: Banks were failing and the economy was in a severe recession. Like President Obama, he brought a Democratic landslide in his wake, with the party establishing comfortable majorities in both houses. Like the Democrats of today, most of those legislators felt that they had been elected to do something radical.

Just as bad policies usually come at times of crisis, so their authors are usually acting from decent motives. I don't question the sincerity of either the New Dealers or their successors today. Roosevelt's supporters genuinely believed that they were standing up for ordinary people against the power of the lobbies and the vested interests—a not wholly unfounded belief, if we are honest. FDR was, after his fashion, a convinced patriot, seeking to rescue what he saw as the victims of a failed laissez-faire system.

The trouble is that the president's moral certainty justified, in his own mind, sweeping aside all opposition, and overturning the checks on his power laid down in the Constitution. Convinced of his own rectitude, he was happy to exceed the powers granted to his office, to rule by executive order, to sidestep the legislature, to trample on the prerogatives of the states, to disregard the two-term convention, and to attempt to pack the Supreme Court.

In the name of combating the recession, the New Dealers unbalanced the Constitution, presiding over an expansion of executive power that was wholly at odds with what the framers had envisaged. And for what?

For a long time, even Roosevelt's critics tended to concede that, while the centralization of political power was regrettable, the New Deal had at least stimulated the economy. Over the past decade, however, the consensus among economists has shifted radically. Many now argue that the New Deal in fact worsened the recession: that it encouraged cartels and crony capitalism, that its regulations burdened businesses that might have led the way to recovery, that its rules on social security and the privileges it granted to labor unions deterred employers from taking on workers.

In 2004, two economists at UCLA, Harold L. Cole and Lee E. Ohanian, conducted a major study that concluded that the New Deal had in fact prolonged the recession by seven years.

According to Professor Cole:

President Roosevelt believed that excessive competition was responsible for the Depression by reducing prices and wages, and by extension reducing employment and demand for goods and services. So he came up with a recovery package that would be unimaginable today, allowing businesses in every industry to collude without the threat of antitrust prosecution and workers to demand salaries about 25 percent above where they ought to have been, given market forces. The economy was poised for a beautiful recovery, but that recovery was stalled by these misguided policies.

It is hard to argue with the proposition that much of the New Deal would be unimaginable today. One of the emergency measures, for example, was an attempt to raise farmers' incomes by removing food surpluses from the market. In other words, at a time when soup kitchens were short of supplies, the federal government was ordering the destruction of comestible food.

The New Deal Democrats, like many elected representatives today, were in the grip of one of the most dangerous of political fallacies: the idea that, at a time of crisis, the government's response must be proportionate to the degree of public anxiety. "Doing nothing is not an option!" intone politicians, as though hyperactivity were itself a solution. Is that phrase ever true? Doing nothing ✓ is always an option, and often it is the best option.

The Roosevelt administration certainly was active: It generated legislation at an unprecedented rate, and created an alphabet soup of new federal agencies: the Resettlement Administration, the Public Works Administration, the Works Progress Administration, the Reconstruction Finance Corporation, and many more.

FDR is the author of the current constitutional dispensation: one that vests far more power in the White House than ever the founders intended. The architecture that he put in place was substantially enlarged by Lyndon B. Johnson, who had started out as a New Deal apparatchik, running the National Youth Administration in Texas. There was some marginal retrenchment during the Reagan years, although federal expenditure went on growing in both relative and absolute terms. But the Gipper was, as so often, the exception. Federal power continued to expand under

George W. Bush, especially in the fields of public education and national security.

———

Looking at the legacy of the New Deal, several lessons seem especially apt to America's present situation.

First, federal agencies and programs are much easier to establish than to discontinue. Many of the bodies established during the 1930s were soon redundant. Some failed even in their immediately declared objectives. Yet it took decades before they were wound up, and several of them still exist, for example the Federal National Mortgage Association: Fannie Mae.

Second, although government spending can have a short-term stimulating effect, state agencies are unwieldy organizations. Often, the worst of the downturn will be over before their full fiscal impact is felt. In consequence, instead of having a counter-cyclical effect, they end up having a *pro*-cyclical effect, generating most of their activity once the recovery has started.

Third, the debt incurred by supposed contingency measures can take decades to pay off, as notionally emergency policies become a permanent drain on the treasury.

Fourth, there is a tendency for governments to expand at times of crisis, not in order to meet the crisis, but in order to allow politicians to demonstrate that they are "doing everything in their power."

Fifth, such expansion is most damaging and most ✓
permanent when it is carried out at a time of one-party
dominance.

Sixth, whatever the economic consequences of state
expansion, there are always deleterious democratic consequences, as the advantages of decentralization are
lost. Citizens find that the decisions that impact most
tangibly upon them are often taken, not by locally
elected officials, but by the appointed directors of large
bureaucracies.

I'm sure you can see where this argument is going.
The financial crisis of 2008 also prompted governments
around the world to react by extending their powers—
nowhere more so than in the United States and the
United Kingdom. The leaders of those countries, doubtless from the best of motives, believed that governments could ward off recessions by spending more,
borrowing more, owning more, and regulating more.

The trouble is that the pursuit of these policies has
left their peoples poorer and less free. The story of the
Roosevelt years should stand as a warning to Americans
of the extent to which one administration can fundamentally alter the relationship between state and citizen, trampling over the founders' vision and making
permanent and harmful changes to the republic. Let's
hope that this generation doesn't need to be taught that
lesson again.

5

DON'T COPY
EUROPE

To the size of a state there is a limit, as there is to plants,
animals and implements, for they can none of them retain
their natural facility when they are too large.

—ARISTOTLE

American journalists are forever trying to get me to be
disobliging about President Obama. It's not something
I want to do, for several reasons.

First, etiquette. The chap is your head of state, the
supreme representative and exemplar of a great nation.
There's a decorum about these things.

Second, diplomacy. Politicians shouldn't be critical
of foreign leaders without very good reason.

Third, democracy. Barack Obama won a handsome
electoral mandate, and many good, generous, patriotic
Americans—Americans such as my cousins in Philadelphia, of whom I'm tremendously fond—voted for him.

Fourth, decency. He seems a likeable fellow, with a
wonderful family to whom he is plainly devoted.

Fifth, benefit of the doubt. I don't believe for a moment that any U.S. president would deliberately set out to impoverish his country, or to undermine its essential freedoms. If these outcomes should ensue, they are likely to be the unintended consequences of well-intentioned reforms.

The sixth consideration, however, towers over the first five. No friend of the United States wants an American president to fail. The security and prosperity of the world are underpinned by the strength of the United States.

Friendship carries obligations. When you see a friend about to repeat your mistakes, you try to warn him. Let me, then, offer this chapter in a spirit of amity. I have been a Member of the European Parliament for eleven years. I am living in your future. Let me tell you a few things about it.

DON'T EUROPEANIZE THE ECONOMY

President Obama, not unreasonably, wants to reconcile America to Europe. Indeed, he didn't wait to be elected before setting to work. During the 2008 campaign, he promised a crowd of giddy Berliners that he would reaffirm America's support for multilateralism, for European integration, and for concerted action against global warming.

Immediately after assuming office, he toured European capitals to repeat these themes. "America has been arrogant," he told delighted audiences. He would be different. He would propose cuts in the stocks of nuclear weapons. He would support the Rio-Kyoto-Copenhagen process. He would embrace a more European model of health care and social security. And, not least, he would support the process of political integration in the EU: "In my view there's no Old Europe or New Europe," he told a NATO summit in Prague, silkily repudiating Donald Rumsfeld's distinction. "There is a united Europe."

The Euro-elites—as opposed to their Euro-skeptic populations—were overjoyed. For the avoidance of doubt, Obama rammed home his point: "I believe in a strong Europe, and a strong European Union, and my administration is committed to doing everything we can to support you."

It is only fair to note that Obama balanced his apologies by chiding European anti-Americans—although, for whatever reason, this part of his message was not widely reported in Europe.

Of course, there is nothing wrong with a U.S. president trying to make his country more popular. On the contrary, it's a vital part of his job. President Obama is a fine orator, and it would have been remiss of him not to seek to capitalize on the goodwill generated by his election. If all he was doing was listening more sympathetically, explaining America's position more coherently and seeking to win new allies through personal diplomacy, I hope all Americans would support him.

The alarming thing is that President Obama, the former chair of the Senate's Europe Committee, seems genuinely to believe that the United States can usefully learn from the European political and social model. The platform on which he was elected, and the policies he is now implementing, are not a series of solitary initiatives lashed randomly together. They amount to a sustained project of Europeanization: state health care, government day care, universal college education, carbon taxes, support for supra-nationalism, bigger government, a softer foreign policy.

Of course European leaders are flattered by the mimicry. But, in their heart of hearts, even *they* know that pursuing such an agenda leaves a country less prosperous and less free.

In eleven years in Brussels and Strasbourg, I have seen at close hand what the European model is, how it works, and what its unintended consequences are. Mr. President, before you rush into anything, please take a closer look at where Europeanization leads.

First, consider the big picture. It is true that, between 1945 and 1974, Western Europe generally outperformed the United States, and the idea of a "European economic model" draws on a folk memory of this era.

National stereotypes, for some reason, persist long after the reality has passed. You will often still be told that British food is terrible, that Germans are militaristic, that Americans are rough frontiersmen. All these things once may have been true, but they are not true now.

So it is with the supposed success of the Rhineland model of cooperative Euro-capitalism, which it was once fashionable to call "the social market." Since 1974, the United States has comprehensively outgrown the EU. Indeed, between 1980 and 1992, if you exclude the United Kingdom, the EU failed to create a single net new private sector job. And the relative sluggishness of the Old World has continued to this day: slow growth, high taxes, short working days, structural unemployment.

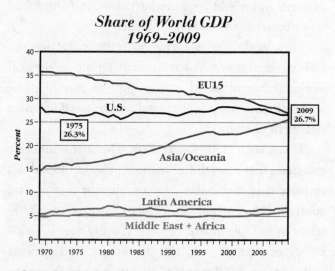

Share of World GDP
1969–2009

Source: Economic Research Service of the U.S. Department of Agriculture

EU leaders recognize that the U.S. economy is more dynamic than their own, and occasionally issue staccato statements to the effect that they really ought to do something about it. In 2000, for example, they committed themselves to something called the Lisbon Agenda, designed to give the EU "the most dynamic and competitive knowledge-based economy in the world capable of sustainable economic growth with more and better jobs and greater social cohesion, and respect for the environment by 2010."

Well, here we are in 2010 and, sure enough, capital has continued to migrate from Europe to the genuinely dynamic and competitive knowledge-based economies of Asia. The EU's share of world GDP has shrunk by 4 percent, and would have contracted much further had it not been for an influx of migrants.

Then again, no one ever really believed that the Lisbon Agenda would have much impact in the real world. It was intended in the spirit of one of those Soviet slogans about higher production: a Stakhanovite statement of intent.

The French philosopher René Descartes famously imagined that everything we thought we could see was in fact being manipulated by a malicious demon who controlled our senses. Eurocrats evidently see themselves in the role of that demon. The EU they describe is one of high growth, full democracy, and growing global influence. But this EU exists only in European

Commission communiqués, in European Council press releases, in European Parliament resolutions.

European legislation has become declamatory: a way to "send a message" or to show that the people passing it care very much about a subject. It is no longer expected to connect with the real world.

I have lost count of how many times I have had variants of the following conversation with my fellow MEPs or with Commission officials:

Hannan: "We have a serious problem with unemployment."

Eurocrat: "Nonsense. Look at the resolution we adopted last month. The fight against unemployment is one of our top three priorities."

Hannan: "Yes, but our regulations on working hours, statutory works councils, paternity leave, and temporary workers are deterring employers from taking people on."

Eurocrat: "Didn't you hear what I just said, Hannan? *One of our top three priorities!*"

Not all EU leaders engage in self-deception, of course. Many of them privately accept that, taking everything together, the American economy is stronger and more dynamic than their own. But this, they tell themselves, is a price well worth paying for Europe's quality of life.

A European worker need not fear sickness or unemployment as his American counterpart does, they argue. He enjoys more leisure time, with shorter working days and longer vacations.

This is certainly true. It now takes four Germans to put in the same number of man-hours as three Americans: The average German works 1,350 hours a year to the American's 1,800. Indeed, the right to time off has now been enshrined in the European Constitution (see chapter 3):

"Every worker has the right to limitation of maximum working hours, to daily and weekly rest periods and to an annual period of paid holiday."

The EU as a whole has adopted a statutory maximum working week of forty-eight hours. Some member states have gone further: In France, for example, it is prohibited to work for more than thirty-five hours a week.

Forty-eight hours might not sound unreasonable. But consider the bureaucracy involved. Almost every business in my constituency makes the same complaint. It's not that they require their employees to work more than forty-eight hours, save for rare and exceptional periods, such as when rushing to meet an order. What they object to is having to prove, to the satisfaction of the government, that they are complying with the regulation. They have to keep time logs. They have to store paperwork. They have to take days off in order to explain themselves to inspectors. For large corporations with full-time personnel managers, these duties are an irritant. But for small firms operating within tight profit margins, they can make the difference between profitability and insolvency.

Understandably, many European businesses are wary about hiring people. In a lightly regulated market, employers will gladly take on more staff during the boom years, knowing that they will be able to lay them off if things go wrong. But as employees become both more expensive (through higher social security contributions, accrued rights, and other benefits) and harder to fire (because small employers cannot afford to go repeatedly before employment tribunals), bosses make the rational decision to have as small a payroll as possible.

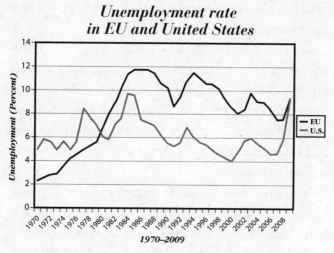

Unemployment rate in EU and United States

1970–2009

Sources: IMF World Economic Outlook, Eurostat

Here, essentially, is Europe's economic tragedy. It suffers no worse than the United States during recessions. But it fails to recover to the same extent during the intervening upswings. As a result, the EU is dwindling. While the U.S. share of world GDP has held steady for forty years, that of Old Europe—the fifteen states that were already in the EU prior to the admission of the former Comecon nations—has declined sharply. And, on current projections, it is expected to decline more sharply still: from 26 percent today to 15 percent in 2020. (Be aware of one statistical trick, incidentally: Projections that show the EU's share of world GDP holding steady, or declining only slightly, are based on the presumption that more and more countries will join, which, even if it happened, would raise economic output only in absolute, not proportionate, terms.)

I often cite the growth figures when my Euro-colleagues tell me that Europeans have simply made a lifestyle choice. "Let the Americans work like drones," they say. "Let them go without health insurance and social protection. Let them gobble sandwiches at their desks instead of having a proper two-hour lunch. There is more to life than GDP."

La dolce vita is defensible enough in the short term. Long weekends, statutory sick leave, paid vacations: What's not to like? The trouble is that, eventually, reality imposes itself. Europe's boom years—the 1950s and 1960s, the years of the German *Wirtschaftswunder*, or "economic miracle"—were, as we can see in retrospect, a bounce back from the ruin of World War II. Europe happened to enjoy perfect conditions for rapid growth.

Infrastructure had been destroyed, but an educated, industrious, and disciplined workforce remained. There was also, for the first time in Europe's history, mass migration. Within individual nations, people moved in unprecedented numbers from the countryside to the growing cities. Within Europe, they journeyed from the Mediterranean littoral to the coalfields and steelworks of northern Europe. And millions more came from beyond Europe—from North Africa, Turkey, and the former British, French, and Dutch colonies.

As if all these advantages were not enough, Europe received a massive external stimulus. Thirteen billion dollars were disbursed through the Marshall Plan between 1948 and 1952, on top of the twelve billion already given by the United States in aid since the end of the war. Colossal as these transfers were by the standards of the time, Europe was receiving an even more valuable gift in the form of the U.S. security guarantee. The defense budgets of most Western European states were, as a percentage of GDP, around a quarter of that of the United States (Britain and France were exceptions). The money that was freed up by low military spending could be spent instead on civil programs.

In the circumstances, it would have been extraordinary had Europe *not* prospered. Human nature being what it is, however, few European leaders attributed their success to the fact that they were recovering from an artificial low, still less to external assistance. They persuaded themselves, rather, that they were responsible for their countries' growth rates. Their genius, they thought, lay in having hit upon a European "third way" between the excesses of American capitalism and the totalitarianism of Soviet Communism.

They believed in markets, but regulated markets. Instead of the industrial strife that they had experienced before the war, they would establish a tripartite system in which employers, labor unions, and government officials worked together. Instead of see-sawing between left and right, they would have consensual coalition governments, in which both Christian Democrats and Social Democrats accepted the broad framework of a mixed social market. Instead of competition between states, they would pursue political and economic integration.

We can now see where that road leads: to burgeoning bureaucracy, more spending, higher taxes, slower growth, and rising unemployment. But an entire political class has grown up believing not just in the economic superiority of Euro-corporatism, but in its moral superiority. After all, if the American system were better—if people and businesses could thrive without government supervision—there would be less need for politicians. As Upton Sinclair once observed, "It is difficult to get a man to understand something when his job depends on not understanding it."

Americans, however, have no such excuse. You have the evidence before your eyes. It's not that everything

European is bad and everything American is good—far from it. It's that the bits of the European model that are most visibly failing are the bits that you seem intent on copying: a larger government role in health care and social security, state ownership of key enterprises, from banks to the auto industry, regulation of private salaries, higher state spending, and political centralization.

DON'T EUROPEANIZE HEALTH CARE

Let me—perhaps recklessly, in the circumstances—return to the example of health care. In August 2009, I was asked on Fox News whether I'd recommend the British health-care model to Americans. I replied that, if you look at international comparisons, Britain fares badly. Our waiting times are longer than in other Western nations, and our survival rates are lower. Britain is pretty much the last place in the industrialized world where you'd want to be diagnosed with cancer, stroke, or heart disease.

This wasn't because of any failing on the part of our medical professionals, I said. Many wonderful people became doctors and nurses because they wanted to help others. But the system didn't maximize their potential. Unlike most European health-care systems, where there is a mix of state and private provision, the British system is monolithic: Everything is run by the government and funded out of general taxation.

The British National Health Service, I added, was the third largest employer in the world behind the People's Liberation Army in China and Indian Railways, employing 1.3 million people. Yet the doctors and nurses were a minority within that 1.3 million: They were outnumbered by administrative and other non-medical staff.

I joked that simply to say what I was saying would open me to attacks in Britain. I would be accused of "insulting our hardworking doctors and nurses"—when, in fact, the employees of the NHS stand to gain more than anyone else from the end of a system that allows the state ruthlessly to exploit its position as a monopoly employer.

It didn't take long for my jocular prediction to be fulfilled. A few days after my return to the United Kingdom, Labour politicians went into overdrive. It was "unpatriotic," said Health Minister Andy Burnham, to criticize the NHS in front of a foreign audience (this from a party that has systematically handed away Britain's powers of self-government in defiance of popular opinion and in breach of its own manifesto promise of a referendum). The Prime Minister, Gordon Brown, dedicated a passage of his speech to the Labour conference to excoriating me. The main Labour newspaper, *The Daily Mirror*, trotted out the very cliché that

I had forecast: I had, it said, "insulted our hardworking doctors and nurses."

I recount this episode for a reason. The point that I had been trying to make in the United States was that once politicians assume responsibility for health care, they find that they have made an almost irreversible decision, and one which, over time, will open taxpayers to unlimited liabilities. Whatever the economic situation, it will be politically impossible to stop increasing the health-care budget, because doing so will lead to accusations of leaving dangerously ill people untended. Every British political party fought the 2010 election on the basis that there would have to be spending reductions in order to contain the deficit, and every one had to tack on an exemption, promising to increase spending on the NHS.

More to the point, it becomes almost impossible to suggest any reform, because the slightest criticism of the system is howled down as an attack on the people who work in it.

Nigel Lawson, Margaret Thatcher's Chancellor of the Exchequer, wrote after leaving office:

> *The National Health Service is the closest thing the English have to a religion, with those who practice in it regarding themselves as a priesthood. This made it quite extraordinarily difficult to reform. For a bunch of laymen, who called themselves the Government, to presume to tell*

*the priesthood that they must change their ways in any re-
spect whatever was clearly intolerable. And faced with a
dispute between their priests and ministers, the public
would have no hesitation in taking the part of the priesthood.*

Britain thus finds itself in a paradoxical situation.
Every day, the newspapers carry horror stories about
what happens in hospitals. We read of people traveling
abroad for treatment, of thousands of deaths from in-
fections picked up in wards, of potentially life-saving
drugs being withheld on grounds of cost rationing. Yet
no one is allowed to suggest a connection between
these outcomes and the system that produces them. Do
that, and you're "insulting our hardworking doctors
and nurses."

Privately, of course, many doctors and nurses believe that the NHS needs a fundamental overhaul. Following my Fox interview—which, partly because it fell
during the August "silly season," was the leading news
story in the United Kingdom—I received two sorts of
e-mails: those from people who agreed, and who often
recounted horror stories of their own; and those that
asserted that I was a heartless Tory who wanted poor
people to be left to die "as happens in America." While
there were several NHS administrators in the latter
camp, most of the doctors I heard from were in the
former.

For what it's worth, I think there are ways in which the United States could usefully improve its health-care system. The current setup, partly because of the costs ✓ of litigation, is more expensive than it needs to be, and gives too much power to the insurance companies. But the one thing certain to be bigger and more remote than a big and remote insurance company is the federal government.

My own preference is for a system of individual health-care savings accounts, along the lines of what happens in Singapore. Singaporeans are obliged to pay a percentage of their earnings into a dedicated account, a small component of which must go to insure against catastrophic illness, but the bulk of which is used to pay for everyday health-care needs. Because the insurance companies have a much reduced role, health-care providers are encouraged to offer their services as cheaply as possible. Consumers, for their part, also find that thrift is rewarded: Once their savings pot reaches a certain size, they are no longer required to pay anything into it.

A consequence is that, unlike insurance-based systems, the Singaporean model incentivizes healthy activity. Instead of relying on expensive statins, for example, Singaporeans have every reason to improve their diet and exercise. The result? Singapore has a healthier population than that of the United States or Britain, with higher longevity, for less than a quarter of the price:

Health care accounts for 3.5 percent of GDP in Singapore as opposed to 16 percent in the United States.

Incidentally, it is worth stressing that in Singapore, as in every developed nation, the government pays for the health care of those who would otherwise go untreated. Its calculation is that if it concentrates on the poor, rather than trying to run a system for everyone, the poor will be better looked after—partly because the state is devoting its attention to them alone, but mainly because those on low incomes will nonetheless benefit from the general rise in standards caused by consumer choice and competition. On the measurable evidence, this calculation is correct: Poor Singaporeans are much healthier than poor Britons.

You don't have to be a Democrat to fret about the uninsured in America. You don't have to be a think-tank specialist to come up with better alternatives. You don't have to be an angry populist to feel that the system of litigation, which forces doctors to take out expensive insurance against lawsuits, and pass the costs on to their patients, needs reform. But reform should be approached within the spirit of the U.S. Constitution: that is, with the citizen, rather than the government, taking charge, and respecting the jurisdiction of the fifty states.

Instead, in March 2010, the United States opted for a federal role in directing health care. Not, that is, a federal role in paying for those who would otherwise be unable to afford treatment, but a state-administered system. True, the government option initially will sit alongside private schemes. But this is how state health care began in Canada. After a while, ministers found that, having assumed responsibility for the system, they were more or less obliged to keep expanding it at the expense of the private sector. Within a few years, the Canadian health-care system was close to being a state monopoly, with private insurance almost squeezed out.

The United States is not Canada, of course, and the system adopted by the Obama administration is not the same as either the British or Canadian model. But the principle has now been established that there will be government-run provision—not simply as a safety net for the poor, but as a direct competitor to private alternatives. The system will be funded out of general taxation, with practitioners answering to state officials. I really hope you've thought this through, my friends. Because, believe me, there is no going back.

DON'T EUROPEANIZE WELFARE

The expansion of the state doesn't just reduce economic growth. More damagingly, it tends to squeeze out personal morality. As taxes rise, charitable donations fall. As social workers become responsible for vulnerable citizens, their neighbors no longer look out for them.

Euro-sophists believe that there is something intrinsically immoral about the American system because it fails the destitute. This failure is inferred from the relatively low benefit entitlements received by poor Americans, and from the conditionality of welfare payments. It is a stock phrase of virtually every European politician, regardless of party, that "a society is judged by how it treats the worst off." Plainly, then, there must be something selfish—and possibly also racist—about a people who keep voting for a system that treats the most needy so pitilessly.

It rarely occurs to the critics that there might be better ways to measure the efficacy of a welfare state than by the size of its budget. Indeed, in a truly successful social security system, budgets ought to fall over time as former recipients are lifted into better and more productive lives.

This, of course, was the original rationale for welfare. But it has been almost entirely forgotten in Europe, where dependency has become structural. Benefits that were intended to have a one-time, transformative effect have instead become permanent, as recipients arrange their affairs around qualifying for subventions. Millions have become trapped in the squalor of disincentives and low expectations. In Britain, which is by no means as badly off as many EU members, the annual welfare budget, including the lump sum payments that, as in the United States, are called "tax credits," comes to more than $200 billion a year. Yet this huge contribution has little impact on either poverty or inequality.

It's the same story elsewhere in Europe: Paying ✓ people to be poor has created more and more poor people.

The United States is different, and different for reasons that, again, can be traced back to the DNA encoded at Philadelphia.

In 1996, President Clinton signed into law a reform package that had been proposed by the Republicans in Congress. It stands as the only meaningful overhaul of social security anywhere in the world, succeeding on every measurable indicator. Poverty, unemployment, and welfare budgets fell sharply, while satisfaction among former benefits claimants soared.

It is true that the 1996 act was passed at a time of strong economic growth; but this alone does not explain the almost miraculous shift from dependency to gainful work. The number of families on welfare fell from 5 million to 2 million, and 1.6 million children were taken out of poverty. And, perhaps most impressive, the reforms lifted groups who had been untouched by every previous welfare initiative: Poverty among black children fell from 42 to 33 percent; among single mothers from 50 to 42 percent.

So what was the magical formula? What wand did President Clinton wave to conjure so extraordinary a transformation? Essentially, he devolved responsibility. The 1996 Personal Responsibility and Work Opportunity Act shifted social security from the federal government to the states, and gave local authorities incentives to reduce their caseloads. Offered the freedom to experiment, the states seized it with gusto. Some incentivized employers to take on the workless; others organized schemes themselves; most made the receipt of benefits conditional on taking up job offers. Best practice quickly spread, as states copied what worked elsewhere.

At the same time, no state could afford to carry on as before, signing checks with a minimum of questions asked. Doing so would, as legislators well understood, make such a state a magnet for every bum in America. There was, in short, a measure of healthy competition.

It cannot be stressed too strongly that, without U.S. federalism, the 1996 reforms couldn't have happened. The Gingrich Republicans were able to draw on successful examples from around the country. The policy was made bottom-up rather than top-down.

Prior to the 1996 welfare reform act, a handful of states had developed pilot projects, to which congressional Republicans could point. When critics of the legislation, led by Senator Ted Kennedy, warned that if states were granted greater autonomy, they would cut benefits and services in order to drive the impoverished across the state lines, Republicans were able to reply with one word: "Wisconsin."

Wisconsin had seen its welfare caseloads drop by almost 70 percent between 1987 and 1997, while caseloads in the rest of the country rose steeply. By 2004 almost 67 percent of Wisconsin welfare recipients were working. Wisconsin did not deport the unemployed; it spent 45 percent more per family and found them jobs, self-respect, and a sense of personal empowerment. Wisconsin, in other words, was a living, thriving refutation of those who opposed the devolution program.

Under the Wisconsin regime, claimants were individually evaluated to measure their employability. In each category, they were held accountable for their performance; if they failed to complete their required activities, they were sanctioned. For example, if they failed to show up for work, they faced financial penalties. Appeal processes were put into place to prevent abuse of the system by either recipients or caseworkers. Rather than balking at this raised level of responsibility and accountability, a large number of recipients liked the system, reporting increased self-esteem and hopefulness for the future—to the undisguised incredulity of the European journalists who were periodically dispatched to the lake-ringed state to describe its supposedly Dickensian conditions.

Once all states were allowed to develop their own approaches, some naturally went further. Perhaps the most successful was Florida, which did not merely tweak the former system, but introduced an entirely new social contract for the poor. While the Florida reform reflected major American trends in welfare reform (including time limits on benefits and work requirements), its major contribution to welfare policy was its emphasis on local control and local accountability.

Florida legislators understood that what worked in one part of the state would not necessarily work in another. Special consideration needed to be given to each community's particular needs. Policies designed to help those in tourism-based Miami wouldn't work for those living in small agricultural towns like Immokalee.

Accordingly, Florida created twenty-four regional boards to develop and execute welfare services in their local regions. Floridians had applied the logic of the 1996 act, and taken the federal vision of the framers to its logical conclusion. If the devolution of social security to states worked, they reasoned, its further devolution to sub-units would work better. They were right.

The advantages of localism in welfare are easily listed.

First, large bureaucracies create unintended consequences. Where states and counties can tailor their policies to suit local needs, a uniform system that covers 300 million people is bound to contain loopholes, tempting into dependency some who were never envisaged as claimants.

Second, proximity facilitates discernment. Person A may be a deserving widow who has been unlucky, while person B is a layabout. Local caseworkers may see this clearly. But if the universal rules handed down from Washington place the two applicants in the same category, they must be treated identically.

Third, pluralism spreads best practice. The freedom to innovate means that states can come up with ideas that Washington never would have dreamed of.

Fourth, non-state agents—churches, charities, businesses—are likelier to involve themselves in local projects than in national schemes, and such organizations are far better at taking people out of poverty than are government agencies.

Fifth, localism transforms attitudes. In Europe, many see benefit fraud as cheating "the system" rather than cheating their neighbors. People would take a very different attitude toward, say, the neighbor whom they knew to be claiming incapacity benefit while working as an electrician if they felt the impact in their local tax bill.

Finally, and perhaps most important, localism undergirds the notion of responsibility: our responsibility to support ourselves if we can, and our responsibility to those around us—not an abstract category of "the underprivileged," but visible neighbors—who, for whatever reason, cannot support themselves. No longer is obligation discharged when we have paid our taxes. Localism, in short, makes us better citizens.

Which is why it is such a pity to see that the 1996 legislation has now been eclipsed. In all the fuss about the stimulus package of February 2009, its most damaging provisions were barely reported. Under the guise of contingency, Washington has casually reassumed control of welfare spending. The reforms are over. America is drifting back to dependency.

DON'T EUROPEANIZE SOCIETY

Europeans and Americans approach social policy from different perspectives. In Europe, government action is considered morally preferable to individual benevolence. The former allows poor people to claim an entitlement that is theirs by right. The latter demeans them by obliging them to take charity.

The United States, until very recently at any rate, has remained faithful to what I identified in chapter 1 as the Miltonian vision of liberty: the belief that virtue cannot be coerced. Thus, choosing to make a donation is meritorious, whereas having your contribution forcibly taken from you through taxation and spent on your

behalf robs you of the opportunity to have acted mor- ✓
ally.

The European conception, of course, can easily de-
scend into equating decency with high taxes. It can also
make the related mistake of assuming that the level of
welfare payments is the measure of a society's collective
humanity.

Both assumptions are flawed. I hope I don't need to
persuade readers that private philanthropy is generally
more efficient than taxation, as well as morally preferable. Equally, though, the poor suffer from the assumption that what they need is larger handouts.

Poverty is not simply an absence of wealth. It is
bound up with a series of other factors: family breakdown, substance abuse, poor educational qualifications,
low expectations. It follows that you do not address the
problem of poverty by giving money to the poor. To
take an extreme example, giving $1,000 to a drug addict
is not, in the long term, going to make him better off.
Poverty is best solved holistically, by tackling its con-
tributory conditions.

Sadly, in Europe, the poor generally have been left
to the left, with consequences that, while inconvenient
to the taxpayer, are disastrous for the destitute. Second- ✓
and third-generation welfare claimants are growing up
without any connection to the world of work. For, just
as governments were bad at building cars or installing
telephones, just as they made a poor job of operating

airlines or administering hospitals, so they have made a terrible mess of the relief of poverty.

In assuming monopolistic responsibility for social policy, European states have balefully redefined how their citizens relate to one another. It wasn't so long ago that any adult, seeing a child out of school during term, would stop him and say, "Why aren't you in class?" Now this is seen as the state's duty. It wasn't so long ago that we all kept an eye out for elderly neighbors, and looked to see that they were still collecting their milk bottles each morning. Now this, too, is seen as the government's responsibility. When unusually heavy snow carpeted Europe at the end of 2009, people complained because the authorities were slow to clear their driveways and pavements. Their grandparents simply would have taken out their shovels.

The most damaging aspect of Euro-statism is neither its deleterious economic effects nor its inefficiency, but its impact on the private sphere. As the state has expanded, society has dwindled. Government officials—outreach workers, disability awareness counselors, diversity advisers, inspectors, regulators, licensors, clerks—have extended their jurisdiction. But they have done so at the expense of traditional authority figures: parents, school principals, clergymen.

The state has assumed control over functions that were once discharged within families: health, education, day care, provision for the elderly. So it is perhaps no surprise that the family itself, in Europe, is in decline.

I don't simply mean that the nuclear family has been replaced by a broader diversity of combinations. I mean that there are fewer and fewer babies. The current population of the continent, including European Russia, is around 720 million. According to a UN forecast, that figure will have fallen to 600 million by 2050. Germany's population will fall by 20 million, Russia's by 30 million—a far greater loss than was suffered as a consequence of the Nazi invasion and consequent deportations. The EU's own statistical office, Eurostat, tells a similar story. Within the next fifty years, it expects Germany's population to fall by 14 percent, Poland's by 18—figures that include net immigration.

Total Fertility Rate, 2008

Albania	2.20
Austria	1.41
Belgium	1.82
Bulgaria	1.48
Czech Republic	1.50
Denmark	1.89
Estonia	1.66
Finland	1.85
Germany	1.37

(continued on next page)

(continued from previous page)

Greece	1.45
Hungary	1.35
Italy	1.41
Latvia	1.45
Lithuania	1.47
Luxembourg	1.61
Malta	1.43
Netherlands	1.77
Poland	1.23
Portugal	1.37
Romania	1.35
Slovakia	1.33
Slovenia	1.46
Spain	1.46
Sweden	1.91
United Kingdom	1.94
United States	2.05

Sources: Eurostat and U.S. Census data

Albania is the only European country with what demographers call replacement level fertility: 2.1 or more live births per woman. In every other European state, the population will decline except to the extent that it is offset by immigration. This is not, unlike most forecasts, based on an extrapolation of current trends. The fall in births has already happened: It's a fact. All that remains to us is to decide how to deal with its consequences.

We can also, of course, speculate about its causes. Perhaps the babies are missing because of the spread of contraception and the legalization of abortion. Perhaps the decline has to do with lifestyle changes and the fact that women are settling down at a later age. Perhaps it is simply a function of choice, or of a fashion for smaller units.

The one thing we can say definitively is this: The problem is not nearly so severe in the United States. The number of live births per American woman is almost exactly what demographers estimate to be the rate at which a population will remain stable: 2.1. In Europe, the figure is 1.5.

Can we connect these figures to politics? I think so. What Europeans most disdain in America, especially Red State America, is cultural conservatism. Even those who have little truck with anti-Americanism feel more or less obliged to sneer at America's Christian Right. But I can't help noticing that values voters seem to be keeping up their numbers. Just as the United States is outbreeding Europe, so the Republicans are outbreed- ✓ ing the Democrats. Mega-churches may offend Euro- pean taste, but they have plenty of children in their Sunday schools.

The higher rates of church attendance in the United States are arguably themselves a product of small gov- ernment. The United States was founded on the basis that there would be no state church; instead, there would be friendly competition among congregations. In most of Europe, by contrast, there is either a single state church or a number of approved religious bodies, often in receipt of state funds. In other words, religion in the United States has been privatized: There is a free market of denominations. And privatization, as we know, tends to raise standards across the board. With no state support, American churches compete for worshippers, and worshippers compete to raise their ministers' salaries. At the same time, people tend to be more loyal to what they have chosen than to what they have been allocated.

European countries retain the outward forms of religion. Monarchs mark the key events of their reigns with religious services and bishops participate at state functions, but the cathedrals are empty.

It is perhaps no coincidence that European Muslims, who are less secularized than their neighbors, have commensurately higher birthrates. Albania, which, as I say, is the only European state sustaining its population through natural fecundity, is also the only Muslim state in Europe. I traveled often in Turkey (2.5 live births per woman) when my own children were babies. I discovered that it is quite normal there for passing strangers, of both sexes, to lift toddlers out of their strollers and hold them aloft, declaring delightedly: "Thanks be to God!" I don't want to construct an elaborate theory of demographics on one heartwarming Turkish custom, but might there be a link between birthrates and collective optimism?

Consider the chronology. The major expansion of government in Europe came during World War II; powers seized on a supposedly contingent basis during mobilization generally were retained when peace returned. Exactly a generation later, from about 1970, birthrates plummeted. The first generation raised with cradle to grave welfare, to be excused from the traditional responsibilities of adulthood, was also the first to give up on parenthood. Throughout this period, there was a decline, not only in church attendance, but in the social values that traditional morality had encouraged.

I am not positing a sole and sequential link between these developments. Plainly there are several factors at work, and we should be careful not to oversimplify. But we can say one thing with confidence: Europeans are extraordinarily relaxed about their continent's sterility. If the figures cited by the UN and Eurostat are even vaguely accurate, Europe faces a choice between depopulation and immigration on a scale never before seen. In a healthy polity, you'd expect there to be a lively debate about what to do next. But European voters have long since given up on politics as a means to deliver meaningful change. It's altogether more pleasant to talk about something else.

DON'T EUROPEANIZE IMMIGRATION

In Amsterdam on November 2, 2004, Mohammed Bouyeri, a twenty-six-year-old Dutch Moroccan, shot Theo Van Gogh, a filmmaker and professional pain-in-the-neck, before methodically slicing him open with a machete. He then strolled calmly away, telling a screaming witness, "Now you know what you people can expect in the future."

The fact that Bouyeri, like the murderer of the populist politician Pim Fortuyn eighteen months previously, had pedaled to the crime scene by bicycle, gave the affair a grisly Dutch motif, but the controversy quickly became global.

Most European governments recognized the problem: They, too, had managed to alienate a minority of their second-generation immigrants to the point of driving them into armed revolt.

Over the past decade, dozens of young British men have traveled to Iraq and Afghanistan to take up arms against their fellow countrymen. At least two crossed from the Gaza Strip into Israel as suicide bombers.

Others have been involved in domestic terrorism, notably a bomb attempt on the London Underground.

Whenever one of these cases occurs, critics tend to attribute blame in one of two ways. Some blame Muslims, arguing that they have failed to integrate with Western society. Others blame Western governments for pursuing provocative foreign wars.

To see why neither side is right, consider the story of America's Muslims. There are more practitioners of Islam in America than in Britain, Belgium, and the Netherlands combined. While the United States doesn't keep religious census data, most estimates range between 2.5 million and 4.5 million, depending on how many devotees of the various African American Muslim movements established in the twentieth century are counted as orthodox Muslims.

If those who blame the disaffection of European Muslims on Western foreign policy were right, one would expect a similar disaffection among their American co-religionists. After all, if Britain is damned by radical mullahs for allying itself with the United States, how much more terrible must be the Great Satan itself?

Yet, in the decade since the attacks in New York and Washington on September 11, 2001, repeated surveys have all indicated the same thing: that American Muslims are patriotic, that they feel lucky to be living in the United States, and that, while some complain of discrimination, the overwhelming majority enjoy excellent community relations. Indeed, as the survey below conducted by Pew Research in 2007 suggests, American Muslims are generally more pro-American than their non-Muslim neighbors.

	U.S. MUSLIMS (TOTAL) (PERCENT)	GENERAL PUBLIC (PERCENT)
American Work Ethic		
Can get ahead with hard work	71	64
Hard work is no guarantee of success	26	33
Rate Your Community		
Excellent/Good	72	82
Fair/Poor	27	18
Personal Financial Situation		
Excellent/Good	42	49
Fair/Poor	52	50
Satisfied with State of United States		
Satisfied	38	32
Dissatisfied	54	61
Muslims coming to the United States today should . . .		
Adopt American customs	43	N/A
Try to remain distinct	26	N/A
Both	16	N/A
Neither	6	N/A

The United States, of course, prides itself on its success in integrating newcomers. The country was, in a sense, designed for that purpose, and American nationality, as we saw in chapter 1, has always been a civic rather than an ethnic or religious concept. Anyone can become an American by buying in to American values. It's a heartening creed, and one to which immigrants from every continent have subscribed. As Ronald Reagan put it, in a characteristically upbeat phrase: "Each immigrant makes America more American."

The United States, in short, gives all its citizens, including its Muslim citizens, something to believe in. There is no need to cast around for an alternative identity when you are perfectly satisfied with the one on your passport.

In most of Europe, however, patriotism is seen as outdated and discreditable. The EU is built on the proposition that national identities are arbitrary, transient, and ultimately dangerous. Indeed, even the passports have been harmonized: The stiff blue British passport has been replaced by a floppy purple EU one. European countries make little effort to inculcate national loyalty in their immigrant communities, because they feel no such loyalty themselves. I am not speaking here of the general population, but of the political and intellectual leaders, who have systematically derided and traduced the concept of patriotism for the past forty years.

I can talk with most authority about my own country, although the experience of neighboring European states is comparable. People sometimes talk of British

Islam as if were a new phenomenon. In fact, during the nineteenth century, there were hundreds of millions of British Muslims.

In the early days of World War I, the Cabinet fretted about their loyalty. It was becoming clear that the United Kingdom would soon find itself in a state of war with Ottoman Turkey, then the world's leading Muslim power. "What will be the effect on our Mussulmans in India and Egypt?" asked the Committee of Imperial Defense. The Ottoman Sultan, after all, was not simply the head of the world's most important Muslim state; he was also the Caliph of Islam, Commander of the Faithful.

The question was answered soon enough. The war with Turkey caused most British Muslims no disquiet whatever. On the contrary, they volunteered in the millions, and served with distinction in Europe as well as the Middle East. One or two Egyptian radicals tried to turn the war with Turkey into another anti-colonial argument but, in those days, the idea that there was a tension between a man's religious conviction and his civic loyalty struck most Muslims as bizarre.

What has changed? Two things. First, there have been changes within Islam. The 1979 Iranian Revolution one day will be seen as an epochal event, on a par with the French Revolution of 1789 or the Russian Revolution of 1917. Like them, it immediately burst out from behind its borders, seeking to replicate itself around the world. Like them it refused to recognize the legitimacy of the international order, claiming a higher authority than the law of nations. The ayatollahs did not develop the doctrine that devout Muslims could not be wholly loyal to non-Muslim states, but they popularized it.

Perhaps the more significant change, however, has taken place within Europe. The reason that millions of British Muslims fought for the Crown in two world wars is because Britishness was a powerful brand, an identity they wanted to adopt.

The troubled young men who set out from Beeston and Wanstead and Tipton to become terrorists had been reared by the British welfare state. One might have thought that their great-grandfathers had greater cause to resent the United Kingdom, which had, after all, invaded and occupied their homelands. But, paradoxically, it was precisely this demonstration of power and confidence that facilitated their loyalty.

"Thou must eat the White Queen's meat, and all her foes are thine," Kipling's border chieftain tells his son, "and thou must harry thy father's hold for the peace of the Border-line. And thou must make a trooper tough and hack thy way to power. Belike they will raise thee to Ressaldar when I am hanged in Peshawur!"

Compare that to the experience of a young Muslim growing up in one of Britain's inner cities. To the extent that he was taught any British history, it will have been presented to him as a hateful chronicle of racism and exploitation. Most of his interactions with the state will have taught him to despise it. Nor will he get much encouragement from his country's leaders. As British identity is scorned, the inhabitants of its constituent nations have begun to grope backward toward older patriotisms: Welsh, Scottish, or English. But where does this leave the children of immigrants?

As for the notion that he will feel grateful to the country that provides a generous welfare system, this is wholly to misunderstand human nature. Two of the London Tube bombers had been living on benefits, as many of the radical imams around Europe have always done.

The idea that poverty is a breeding ground for violence and terrorism derives, ultimately, from Karl Marx and, like most of his teachings, it sounds plausible enough until you stop to analyze it. Revolutionary violence, historically, has tended to occur, not at times of deprivation, but at times of rising wealth and aspiration. Put bluntly, people who are worried about where the next meal is coming from have little time for protest marches, let alone bomb-making.

The modern welfare state, by contrast, is the ideal terrorist habitat. It keeps people fed but idle. And, naturally, it makes them resent their paymasters.

Sean O'Callaghan, a former IRA volunteer, recalls talking to the terrorist leader Brian Keenan. "The Brits are very clever," Keenan told him. "The only thing they don't get is the Fenian thing. We speak their language, are the same skin color, live in their council houses, take their dole, and still hate them." But might it not have been precisely because of the council houses and the dole that they hated us? It is one thing to have a quarrel with another people, quite another to have to crawl to your enemies for charity.

To put it another way, had the London Tube bombers not had the option of welfare, they might have found productive jobs, instead of working themselves into a rage against the system that doled out their allowances.

It is the same story across Europe. As national self-confidence has waned, other identities have become more attractive. The Anglo-Dutch writer Ian Buruma has written a magisterial book about the killing of Theo Van Gogh, *Murder in Amsterdam*. While writing it, he toured the "dish cities": the immigrant suburbs that ring Dutch towns, so named for the satellite dishes that connect the inhabitants to their ancestral countries.

Although he hands down few hard conclusions, Buruma offers some intriguing insights. For most Muslims in Europe, the central fact of their identity is not that they are Muslims, but that they are children of immigrants. Like second-generation settlers everywhere, they feel torn between the country where they grew up and the sunlit land of their parents' reminiscences. Some of them become literally schizophrenic:

Personality disorders are ten times more common among second-generation Dutch Moroccans than among the indigenous people.

There is nothing peculiarly Muslim about mild deracination. Every second-generation immigrant feels it, even in America. I was born into the then sizeable British community in Lima and remember, as a six-year-old, agonizing over whether to support Peru or Scotland in the 1978 soccer World Cup. True, I never took up arms for the old country, but my father did. Like almost all the Anglo–South American boys of his generation, he left the land of his birth to fight Hitler. No one suggested, on his return, that he no longer had the right to live loyally and peaceably among Peruvians.

Which brings us back to the U.S. experience. Clever and fashionable Europeans mock the profusion of flags on American porches. When anti-Americans express themselves through posters or cartoons, they do so by parodying the symbols of American patriotism: red-white-and-blue bunting, Uncle Sam, stars-and-stripes hats. Yet it is these expressions of national togetherness—or, rather, the sentiment that produces them—that have made the assimilation of immigrants so much more successful than in Europe. As long as Americans believe in themselves, others will believe in them, too. As Toby says of the Muslim radicals in *The West Wing*: "They'll like us when we win."

Certainly that has been the European experience. Confident countries have little difficulty infecting others with their confidence. But when the ruling idea in Europe is that the nation-state is finished, and that we should hand what is left of our sovereignty to the Brussels bureaucracy, it is little wonder that settlers scorn their new homelands.

In order to sustain its population, and to keep the ratio of workers to retirees stable, the EU will absorb perhaps a hundred million immigrants over the next half century. Its leaders can hardly blame them if they ✓ have their own ideas about how to remake society when those leaders themselves seem to offer nothing better.

DON'T ABANDON FEDERALISM

The diverse Euro-woes identified in this chapter gush from a single spout. All of them are caused, or at least exacerbated, by the phenomenon of large and remote government. Other things being equal, big and central-ized states are likelier than small and devolved states to: be sclerotic; have more bureaucrats and higher taxes; have soulless and inefficient welfare systems; crowd out ✓ non-state actors, from churches to families; and have fatalistic and cynical electorates.

To put it the other way around, the devolution of power stimulates growth, makes administration more democratic, connects citizens to their nation, and allows a flourishing private sphere: the attribute that Tocqueville most admired about America.

Consider the example of Switzerland, one of the wealthiest and most successful states in Europe. America's Founding Fathers were much taken with the Helvetic Confederation. John Adams admired the way the Swiss had developed universal suffrage and a popular militia. Patrick Henry praised the country for maintaining its independence without a standing army or a "mighty and splendid President."

Switzerland, of course, is made up of twenty-six autonomous cantons. Like the United States, but unlike almost every country in Europe, it makes regular use of referendums as a method of government. In consequence, Swiss voters feel little of their neighbors' political disaffection: They know that their system of direct democracy has served to control their politicians and to constrain the growth of government.

Interestingly, it has also served to foster a strong sense of national identity. Switzerland has four official languages, yet its burghers are united by strong national sentiment. Three times since 1870, France and Germany have fought atrocious wars against each other, but never once did these conflicts spill over into unrest between French- and German-speaking Swiss citizens.

Switzerland, like most European countries, has absorbed a sizeable immigrant population. But direct democracy ensures that Swiss people have a degree of control over whom they are admitting and in what numbers. In some cantons, immigration applications are voted on *as individual cases*: Those seeking naturalization are invited to submit a photograph and a short essay setting out why they should be allowed to stay. Sure enough, the ones allowed in tend to be the ones who have demonstrated their willingness to integrate.

No wonder the Swiss have refused to join the EU. They know that their unique system of dispersed democracy and popular sovereignty would be incompatible with Euro-centralization.

The United States, alas, is going in the opposite direction. It's not a specific policy that worries me, so much as the assumptions that underpin *all* the programs of the present administration. If Washington had decided, in isolation, to reassume control of social security, it would be an error, but a reversible one. If, in response to the financial crisis, there had been a one-time injection of federal spending, I'd still have disagreed, but it would have been a defensible proposition.

The trouble is that these things are not unrelated initiatives. They amount to a sustained and deliberate shift in power: from the states to Washington, from the citizen to the government, from the elected representative to the federal czar. It's no wonder the current administration is so keen on a European superstate: It is constructing its own version at home.

Europeanization is incompatible with the vision of the founders and the spirit of the republic. Americans are embracing all the things their ancestors were so keen to get away from: high taxes, unelected lawmakers, pettifogging rules.

That, of course, is your business as Americans. But it's our business, too. Being the strongest nation on the planet carries certain responsibilities. The world has, until now, been fortunate in its superpower. The promise of the U.S. Constitution didn't simply serve to make Americans free. It also drove your fathers to carry liberty to other continents. A fundamental alteration of the character of the republic is not simply an internal matter: If America Europeanizes its domestic arrangements, it will sooner or later Europeanize its foreign policy, too. At which point, your problems become our problems.

6

AMERICA
IN THE WORLD

In the transaction of your foreign affairs we have endeavored to cultivate the friendship of all nations, and especially of those with which we have the most important relations. We have done them justice on all occasions, favored where favor was lawful, and cherished mutual interests and intercourse on fair and equal terms. We are firmly convinced, and we act on that conviction, that with nations as with individuals our interests soundly calculated will ever be found inseparable from our moral duties, and history bears witness to the fact that a just nation is trusted on its word when recourse is had to armaments and wars to bridle others.

—THOMAS JEFFERSON, 1805

"Americans are from Mars, Europeans are from Venus." Such phrases catch on because they capture a mood, crystallizing what had been until then an inchoate feeling, putting into words thoughts that people hadn't verbalized.

The quotation comes from the opening lines of Robert Kagan's 2003 book, *Of Paradise and Power*. Kagan's treatise was, of course, much more subtle and layered than that slogan suggests. But, in the year that saw the invasion of Iraq, those words transcended the thesis that had generated them, and took on a life of their own.

Throughout the 1990s, the realization had been gradually dawning on Europeans that they no longer needed U.S. military protection. There was no more need even to pretend to defer to the nation whose nuclear guarantee had kept the Red Army from marching to the North Sea. It was possible for Europeans—especially if they banded together—to assert an altogether different foreign policy from that of the *hyper-puissance*.

Different in what ways? Javier Solana, a former socialist minister from Spain who became the first man to aspire to run the EU's foreign policy, defined its peculiar characteristics as follows:

What are the elements? I would say compassion with those who suffer; peace and reconciliation through integration; a strong attachment to human rights, democracy, and the rule of law; a spirit of compromise, plus a commitment to promote in a pragmatic way a rules-based international system. But also a sense that history and culture are central to how the world works and therefore how we should engage with it. When Americans say "that is history," they often mean it is no longer relevant. When Europeans say "that is history," they usually mean the opposite.

You get the picture. Europeans are smart, sophisticated, sensitive. They understand the past. They rely on force of argument, not force of arms. They keep the rules.

Americans, by implication, are the reverse of all these things. They favor *Machtpolitik* over *Moralpolitik*. They throw their weight around. They blunder in, with little sensitivity toward local conditions. They stick to the rules only when it suits them. They are, if not wholly uninterested in democracy and human rights, certainly willing to trample over them in pursuit of immediate gain.

Americans, of course, were at the same time evolving their own converse stereotype. Europeans in general, and Frenchmen in particular, were ingrates, who had accepted American protection for forty years, and were now driven by a pathological need to bite the hand that freed them. As the Euro-enthusiast British writer Tim Garton Ash put it:

> *The current stereotype of Europeans is easily summarized. Europeans are wimps. They are weak, petulant, hypocritical, disunited, duplicitous, sometimes anti-Semitic, and often anti-American appeasers. In a word: "Euroweenies." Their values and their spines have dissolved in a lukewarm bath of multilateral, transnational, secular, and postmodern fudge. They jeer from the sidelines while the United States does the hard and*

dirty business of keeping the world safe for Europeans.
Americans, by contrast, are strong, principled defenders
of freedom, standing tall in the patriotic service of the
world's last truly sovereign nation-state.

The invasion of Iraq confirmed the prejudices of both sides. As Europeans saw it, a clique of neo-cons had told lies about Saddam's weapons program in order to drag the world into a ruinous war, whose true purpose was to establish an American garrison in an oil-rich region and win contracts for Dick Cheney's buddies.

Americans, meanwhile, were shaken by the explosion of anti-U.S. sentiment in countries that they had until then regarded as allies. Even those who had voted against George W. Bush were taken aback to see their head of state portrayed as a worse dictator than Saddam Hussein. Even those who had opposed the invasion didn't much care to see it being described as a Jewish plot ("rootless cosmopolitan," "Zionist," now "neo-con": the code word changes from generation to generation).

Kagan's sound bite attracted a great deal of attention in Europe. It was understood as the dismissive snort of a braggart, a typical example of neo-con swaggering. Needless to say, few of the critics had read the accompanying book. If they had, they would have found that Kagan still believes that there is such a thing as the West, is convinced that Europe and America can and should collaborate to mutual advantage, and lauds the process of European integration as a "miracle" and a "reason for enormous celebration." Indeed, the book's main flaw, as John Fonte of the Hudson Institute points out, is that it takes the EU at its own estimate, failing to understand the extent of its anti-democratic propensities.

Nonetheless, very few Europeans dissented from the essential proposition that there was a fundamental cultural divergence between the United States and the EU, partly reflecting the simple reality of military imbalance, but also rooted in a difference of *Weltanschauung*: of how to look at the world. Both sides, in their own way, agreed. Americans really *did* feel they were from Mars, Europeans that they were from Venus.

People naturally describe the divergence with different adjectives, depending on their point of view. America is prepared to back her ideals with actions, whereas Europe blusters. America stands up to bullies, whereas Europe appeases them. America keeps Europe safe while Europe sneers. Or, to turn it around, America defies international law while Europe tries to lead by example. America reacts to criticism with daisy-cutter bombs, Europe with persuasion. America seeks to pulverize those who disagree, Europe to win them over. Take your pick: It amounts to the same analysis.

The most eloquent European answer to the Kagan thesis came in a book published in 2005 with the startling title *Why Europe Will Run the 21st Century.* Its author, a British think-tanker called Mark Leonard, is on the extreme end of the Euro-integrationist spectrum in Britain, but fairly representative of the political class of the EU as a whole.

His proposition is that world leadership will shift to the EU because of Europe's different understanding of power and interest. Instead of attacking its adversaries, the EU seeks to draw them into a nexus of common interest. Its weapons are not bombs and missiles, but trade accords and human rights codes. The worst threat that it holds over recalcitrant neighbors is not that it will invade them, but that it will ignore them. It was precisely in the hope of attracting the sympathetic attention of Brussels, argues Leonard, that Serbia gave up its war criminals for international trial, that Poland liberalized its abortion law, that Turkey strengthened the rights of its Kurdish minority.

One by one, nations are being drawn into what he calls "the Eurosphere." Balkan and even Caucasian states aspire to eventual membership. And more distant nations—the EU's Mediterranean neighbors in the Maghreb and the Levant, the former colonies of Africa, the Caribbean and the Pacific, and the republics that once made up the USSR—are increasingly dependent on EU trade, aid, investment, and political patronage.

Where Washington simply writes checks to such allies as Colombia, Brussels aims for a complete transformation of society: It encourages democratic and liberal reforms so that the governments of its allies will *want* to support the EU. And because the EU is not a superpower, but a network of states, its rise will not attract envy or encourage the formation of hostile coalitions.

It's a tremendously appealing thesis: taut, logical, and consistent. The trouble is that it isn't true. Once again, we are in the world of the Cartesian malicious demon: an EU that exists between the covers of books, but that bears no relation to the actual one.

The EU, Leonard contends, is a force for "democracy, human rights and the protection of minorities." Really? Where exactly? In Iran, where it is cozying up to murderous ayatollahs who, among other things, recently ordered the execution of a teenage girl? In Cuba, where it has withdrawn its support from anti-Castro dissidents? In China, where it has not only declared its willingness in principle to sell weapons to an aggressive tyranny, but is actively collaborating with the Communists on the creation of a satellite system, designed to challenge the "technological imperialism" of America's GPS? In Palestine, where it's funneling subsidies to Hamas, despite its own ban on funding terrorist organizations? Or perhaps within its own borders, where it has adopted a new constitutional settlement in defiance of the will of its citizens, clearly expressed in referendums?

Leonard writes enthusiastically about the Lisbon Agenda and the EU's competitiveness. But, again, this competitiveness is confined to a virtual world of Commission statements and summit communiqués. In the real world, businesses are struggling with the forty-eight-hour week, the Temporary Workers Directive, the Social Chapter, and the rest of the Euro-corporatist agenda. He goes on to predict that, in addition to its economic might, the EU will evolve a powerful military capacity because joint defense procurement projects will lead to economies of scale. He does not mention the supreme example of such joint procurement, the Eurofighter, perhaps the most useless, over-budget, redundant piece of military hardware ever.

Countries within the EU, he writes, are better off than those outside, such as Norway. Yet Norway has a GDP per capita that is more than twice that in the EU. With high growth and negligible unemployment, Norwegians appear to be managing very nicely without Brussels. Do they lack influence in the world? Hardly. Their diplomats have led the way in brokering peace in the Middle East, Sudan, Sri Lanka, and Southeast Asia.

The Euro-enthusiast thesis requires that you push all such inconvenient facts out of your mind. You are invited to take the EU at its word, rather than looking at its deeds. It is enough, for example, to be told that the Constitution commits the EU to democracy and the rule of law. Never mind that the Constitution of, say, East Germany, made similar noises. We are asked, in short, to engage in a massive collective suspension of disbelief. Is unemployment in the EU high? Never mind: We've just published a resolution condemning it. Is corruption rife? We've just set up a study group to tackle it. As in the old Eastern bloc, the gap between the official version and real life keeps getting wider.

This point cannot be stressed too strongly. All nations, like all individuals, sometimes engage in hypocrisy. And, in a sense, it's a good thing they do: Hypocrisy, after all, is a recognition that you could be doing better, a realization that your actions don't meet your aspirations.

What we see in the EU, however, is something on an altogether different scale: a creed of official self-deceit in which leaders trot out slogans that they don't expect anyone to believe.

———————

Consider the difference in approach to greenhouse gas emissions. I don't want to get into the whole global warming debate, which could fill a book larger than this one. My point isn't about the rights and wrongs of carbon emissions. It's about the connection between rhetoric and reality.

Of all the actions of the Bush administration, the one that attracted the most opprobrium in Europe, more even than the Iraq War, was withdrawing from the Kyoto Protocol. And, sure enough, the United States has since produced about 22 percent more carbon than the treaty had envisaged. But many European countries have worse records. Austria, Denmark, and Spain are among the states that have exceeded their quotas by substantially more than the United States. Yet, for some reason, they have escaped criticism. European sensibility requires that people pretend to go along with these supra-national projects, even if they then do nothing about it.

Which, of course, is what the current U.S. administration is now doing. Climate change science is a complex and difficult field, but we can say with some confidence that the proposed cap-and-trade legislation will have a negligible impact. We can say this because even the strongest supporters of emissions cuts insist that the planet will continue to heat almost to the same extent with the legislation. They support it, in other words, not because they think it will make a significant difference, but as a statement of good intention, a sign that the United States is trying to do the right thing.

The cap-and-trade legislation is a further example of the Europeanization of the United States, but not just in the way that critics usually mean. Its European nature resides not only in the fact that it will lead to more regulation and slower growth but also in the fact that American legislators, like their European counterparts, are now engaging in declamatory lawmaking.

The Atlantic splits over foreign policy partly reflect the extent to which policymakers are prepared honestly to declare their objectives. Every state, one supposes, operates on the basis of both *Realpolitik* and morality. Both the EU and the United States seek to export their values, including human rights and the rule of law, and do so from a combination of selfish and altruistic motives. The difference is that Americans are less likely to euphemize what they do.

There was shock in Europe when Donald Rumsfeld, asked why the United States was using cluster bombs against militants in Afghanistan, replied, "To try to kill them." Most Europeans, certainly in those early days, backed military action against the Taliban. And, of course, they understood that military action involves fatalities. But they didn't like to hear it spelled out.

This difference isn't merely the stuff of diplomatic awkwardness. It goes to the heart of what is wrong with the European project—and of why Americans should be wary about the Europeanization of their own polity. There is an old chestnut about a British civil servant telling a politician, "It might work very well in practice, minister, but it doesn't work in theory." That sentiment has been lifted to become the ruling principle of the EU. Never mind how many unpleasant dictators we cuddle up to. Never mind how casually we disregard democracy within our own borders. We're still the good guys: Just read our latest resolution on human rights.

Words matter more than actions, motives than outcomes. Indeed, the very effectiveness of unilateral U.S.
action can offend European sensibilities. When the
2004 tsunami devastated several countries around the
Indian Ocean, the United States, along with India,
Japan, and Australia, began a massive relief operation,
while the EU held press conferences about surveying
the damage. Clare Short, then the International Aid
Minister in Britain's Labour Government, didn't much
care to see American humanitarian assistance: "I think
this initiative from America to set up four countries
claiming to coordinate sounds like yet another attempt
to undermine the UN," she told the BBC. "Only really
the UN can do that job. It is the only body that has the
moral authority." Never mind that the UN had not, at
that stage, done anything: The moral authority was
what mattered.

Of course, moral authority is best purchased with
someone else's money. I shall never forget the debate in
the European Parliament that followed the 2004 catas-
trophe. MEPs began an aggressive auction to demonstrate their compassion.

"Let's pledge a million euros for immediate disaster
relief," one would say. "A million?" the next would de-
claim. "Pah! We must give at least five million!" "With
great respect to my two colleagues who have just
spoken," a third would say, "I am not sure they grasp
the extent of the devastation. Five million might do as

emergency aid, but the cleanup will cost *a minimum of fifty million.*"

And so it went on, each speaker attracting warm applause from Euro-MPs who felt warm about the fact that they were applauding. Then an Italian Christian Democrat, a gently mannered Catholic, rose with a suggestion. Why didn't we make a personal gesture? Why didn't each colleague contribute a single day's attendance allowance to the relief fund?

Immediately the warmth drained from the room. Those who had been hoarsely cheering the allocation of gazillions of their constituents' money were stony at the thought of chipping in €290 of their own (on top of their salaries and various other perks, MEPs get paid for turning up and signing the attendance register). The poor Italian sat down to one of the most hostile silences I can remember, and the idea was immediately dropped.

Contemplate that scene, and you will descry an elemental truth of politics—indeed, of humanity. People treat their own resources differently from other people's. There are, as Milton Friedman observed, two kinds of money in the world: your money and my money. And, in Brussels, it's all your money.

I can perhaps best summarize what's wrong with European gesture politics by adapting a famous observation by P. J. O'Rourke, who wrote that the only political observation he could confidently make was that

God was a Republican and Santa Claus a Democrat. By the same token, then I suspect that God is a Euro-skeptic, and Santa Claus a Euro-enthusiast.

God comes across a pretty stiff sort, a stickler for rules. He disapproves of waste and extravagance. He dislikes idleness. He has little time for the Utopian schemes and overblown ambitions of His creatures. In fact, when a previous generation of men united behind a presumptuous plan for supra-national integration, He took a very dim view indeed:

> *And the Lord came down to see the city and the tower, which the children of men builded. And the Lord said, Behold, the people is one, and they have all one language; and this they begin to do: and now nothing will be re-strained from them, which they have imagined to do. Go to, let us go down, and there confound their language, that they may not understand one another's speech. So the Lord scattered them abroad from thence upon the face of all the earth: and they left off to build the city.*

Now Santa Claus is a very different proposition. He's jolly and generous and likeable. He might know who's been good and who naughty, but he never does anything about it. Everyone gets the goodies, regardless of desert.

Santa Claus, in short, is preferable to God in every way. Except one. *There's no such thing as Santa Claus.*

Let's take a closer look at the areas where I identified that the EU was failing to actualize its frequently stated commitment to human rights: Iran, Cuba, China, Gaza. In all these cases, there is a sharp divergence between American and European policy. To simplify, American policy is to cold-shoulder the dictators and encourage their democratic opponents, while European policy is to engage with the dictators in the hope of encouraging reform. The United States is chiefly concerned with the ballot box, the EU with regional stability.

Once again, what we see is a consequence of the DNA encoded at Philadelphia; what Richard Dawkins would perhaps call "an extended phenotype." The United States was founded in a democratic revolt against a distant government. Like all nations, it treasures and re-tells its founding story. Unsurprisingly, then, its natural prejudice is toward self-determination and democratic accountability.

Of course, democratic prejudice sometimes gives way to national interest, and the United States has propped up its fair share of unpleasant regimes in Africa, Asia, and Latin America. The best we can say is that there was no self-deception involved: policymakers weighed the competing claims of democracy and self-interest, and consciously chose the latter. As Roosevelt is supposed to have said about the Nicaraguan *caudillo* Anastasio Somoza, "He may be a son-of-a-bitch, but he's our son-of-a-bitch." A similar (and similarly misguided) calculation leads the State Department to support the monstrous dictatorship of Islam Karimov in Uzbekistan, simply because he had the wit, in 2001, to proclaim himself an ally in the war on terror.

These exceptions, however, don't disprove the general rule. From Belarus to Zimbabwe, the overarching ambition of U.S. policy is to foster the emergence of democratic alternatives to tyrannical regimes.

Euro-diplomats, other things being equal, are more nuanced; in Solana's phrase, more "pragmatic." They are readier to engage with autocrats, politically and economically. This is partly because they genuinely believe in the power of dialogue and persuasion. But it is also because they don't have the visceral attachment to democracy that has traditionally characterized the American republic.

We have already seen the way the EU dismisses inconvenient referendum results within its own borders. We have seen the way in which the structures of the EU are intrinsically anti-democratic. Supreme power is vested in the hands of twenty-seven unelected European Commissioners. The servants of such a system, when dealing with, say, Chinese officials, are bound to feel more kinship than the emissaries of a state built on Jeffersonian principles.

If you think I'm exaggerating, consider the career of the EU's first ever foreign minister—or, to give her correct title, the High Representative of the Union for Foreign Affairs and Security Policy—a position created under the European Constitution in December 2009.

Baroness Ashton is a typical product both of the British quangocracy and the Brussels mandarinate. A Labour placewoman, she has never in her whole life taken the trouble to get herself elected to anything. Simply to read her CV is to get a sense of the extent to which Britain is run, as explained in chapter 2, by quangos.

First, Lady Ashton worked for the Campaign for Nuclear Disarmament, going on to become its treasurer. Then she went to the Central Council for Education and Training in Social Work. Then she chaired the Health Authority in Hertfordshire, became a vice president of the National Council for One Parent Families, and was eventually appointed a life peer by Tony Blair—all without facing the voters.

Perhaps understandably, given this background, she displayed little enthusiasm for representative government when she got to the House of Lords. Her main achievement as leader of the House was to steer the Lisbon Treaty through the chamber without conceding the referendum that all three parties had promised in their manifestos.

Nor does the contempt for the ballot box stop there. Baroness Ashton became a European Commissioner in 2008, not because of any special aptitude, but because Gordon Brown was determined to avoid a by-election, and so couldn't send an elected MP. She was then promoted to the foreign affairs position in 2009, again, not because of particular expertise in foreign affairs but because it was generally felt that Labour ought to be compensated over Tony Blair not getting Europe's presidency.

Every chapter of that story negates the democratic principle. Every page would have had Sam Adams and Patrick Henry howling about arbitrary government. To summarize: a lifelong quangocrat was appointed in secret to a position created by a treaty on which the public had been denied a vote.

How can such a foreign minister lecture the Cubans about democratic reform? How can she chide Iran for its rigged ballots? Is it any wonder that Euro-diplomats—who have now, under the same treaty, been formed into a recognized diplomatic corps called the European External Action Service—are less willing that their American counterparts to criticize regimes that are insufficiently democratic?

Once again, both unions are being true to the creeds of their founders. Of course there are exceptions, complications, subtleties. But, in general, the sympathy of the American is with the masses, while the sympathy of the Eurocrat is with the ruling officials, who might not have a perfect electoral mandate, but who do at least have some experience of power—the people, in short, who most resemble his fellow Eurocrats.

Sympathy—in the literal sense of fellow-feeling—is an important factor in diplomacy. Consider the Israel-Palestine dispute. An American politician looking at the Middle East is likely to feel sympathy with Israel as the country that looks most like his own: a parliamentary democracy based on property rights and the rule of law, a state founded in adversity that elected its generals as its first leaders. But to the Euro-sophist, who dislikes "coca-colonialism" and feels that the French farmers who stone McDonald's have a point, things look very different. To him, Israel represents an incursion of precisely the same globalized culture that he resents in America. Just as his sympathy is with the settled European smallholder threatened by Wal-Mart, so it is with the Bedouin in his flowing robes.

In my eleven years in the European Parliament, I have often wondered why Israel seems to provoke anger out of all proportion to its population or strategic importance. It is the subject of endless emergency debates and condemnatory resolutions. The EU takes very seriously its role as the chief financial sponsor and international patron of the Palestinian regime. Americans often put the phenomenon down to anti-Semitism, but this won't quite do. There *are* anti-Semites in Europe, of course, but many of those who are angriest in their denunciations of the Jewish state have honorable records of opposing discrimination at home.

So why does Israel find it so much harder to get a fair hearing in Brussels than in Washington? Partly because the EU sees its role as being to counterbalance the United States. Partly, too, because of demographics: We are forever hearing about the "Jewish lobby" on Capitol Hill, but it is rarely mentioned that there are more than four times as many Muslims in the EU as there are Jews in the United States.

The single biggest disadvantage that Israelis have in Brussels, however, is one that they can't do anything about. The story of Israel represents the supreme vindication of the national principle: that is, of the desire of every people to have their own state. For two thousand years, Jews were stateless and scattered, but they never lost their aspiration for nationhood: "Next year in Jerusalem." Then, one day, astonishingly—providentially, we might almost say—they achieved it.

Looked at from an American perspective, it's a heartening story. But, to a convinced Euro-integrationist, national feelings are transient, arbitrary, and ultimately discreditable. Simply by existing, Israel challenges the intellectual basis of the European project. As one Christian Democratic MEP put it in a recent debate,

"Why is Israel building walls when the rest of us are pulling them down?"

To be fair, the EU is being entirely consistent. It is doing precisely what many Europeans criticized the United States for seeking to do in Iraq and Afghanistan. It is doing what the Jacobins did when they took up arms against the old monarchies, what the Russian revolutionaries did when they declared war against the capitalist system, what the Iranian radicals do when they sponsor Islamist militias from the old Silk Road khanates to the Balkans. It is seeking to export its ideology.

The key component of this ideology is transnational integration, which Euro-diplomats prize above virtually every other goal, including democracy. When Slovenia declared its independence from the Yugoslav federation in 1991, following an overwhelming referendum result, the EU condemned the decision and cautioned the other Yugoslav republics against secession. To this day, the EU runs protectorates in Bosnia-Herzegovina and Kosovo, more or less for the sole purpose of preventing partition. Full democracy in those places would lead to ethnographic boundaries, with the Serbian minorities opting for autonomy or union with Serbia (as, in practical if not legal terms, they already have). Faced with a choice between democracy and supra-nationalism, the EU will always choose supra-nationalism.

Why should this bother Americans? Partly because the policy is wrong in itself, clashing as it does with the

United States' commitment to democratic self-determination. Mainly, though, because the EU isn't only imposing multiethnic states on the Balkans. It isn't just encouraging other continents to form supra-national blocs, and making its trade and aid deals conditional on participation therein. It is also seeking to replicate that model at a global level, to trammel and contain the will of sovereign democracies through international bureaucracies.

––––––––––

Robert Bork, whose nomination to the U.S. Supreme Court was blocked by the Senate in 1987, has studied the ballooning of international jurisprudence since the early 1990s, and concluded that it amounts to a sustained attempt to impose on states from above laws and values that would never have passed through their national parliaments.

"What judges have wrought is a coup d'état," he wrote in *Coercing Virtue: The Worldwide Rule of Judges*, "slow-moving and genteel, but a coup d'état nonetheless."

Bork, of course, was mainly concerned about this process at an international level. But it is important to understand where the international phenomenon—a phenomenon from which the United States is not completely immune—originates. Once again, we find that the EU is internationalizing its internal values and norms, in a way that Americans cannot afford to ignore.

I once shared a platform with Judge Bork and suggested that, if the U.S. government were looking to make budgetary savings, it might stop paying the airfares of American judges who attend international legal conferences, whence they return with strange ideas about jurisprudence. Judge Bork considered this for a moment and then replied.

"How about a more moderate proposal: We could pay their airfares *out* . . ."

Europeans cannot get used to the idea that American judges are elected: They consider the whole idea monstrously populist, and complain vigorously about "the politicization of the judiciary." An impartial assessment of European judges, however, will show that they are, if anything, more political than Americans; they simply are not elected.

All of us have our assumptions and our prejudices. Judges don't stop being human beings when they join the bench. But, unless they are elected, they don't have to justify or explain their prejudices to the general population.

It is striking that, in Britain and in Europe, judges tend to be well to the left of public opinion, with the consequence that judicial activism happens overwhelmingly in the same political direction. For example, courts are forever stepping in to block deportation orders: Britain's prisons teem with foreign radicals whom the government is desperate to repatriate, but whom judges will not allow to be removed lest they face torture abroad. I cannot think, though, of a single converse case, where a judge has demanded the removal of an illegal entrant who had improperly been granted leave to remain.

Likewise, whenever a minister steps in to order that a prisoner serve a minimum sentence, judges line up to demand that the independence of the courts be protected from vote-grabbing politicians. But the reverse doesn't apply. When, for example, in a quite blatant interference with judicial process, the government ordered the release of loyalist and republican terrorists under the 1998 Belfast Agreement, not a single judge complained.

Maximum sentences for certain offenses? Absolutely fine. Minimum sentences? An outrageous attempt by politicians to tether the courts.

Judges, in short, can make tendentious and imaginative interpretations of the law in order to advance an agenda that has been rejected at the ballot box.

It is this process that has been globalized. And, at the international level as at the national level, the judicial activism invariably comes from the same direction. The past decade has seen writs served, not only against dictators such as Augusto Pinochet, but against Ariel Sharon, Donald Rumsfeld, and other controversial conservatives. In 2009, Tzipi Livni had to cancel an engagement in the United Kingdom because of an outstanding warrant. Oddly, though, no one ever tried to indict Yasser Arafat, Fidel Castro, or Robert Mugabe.

The internationalization of criminal justice has been one of the main drivers of judicial activism within states. When judges can find no domestic statute to justify the rulings they would like to make, they reach instead for the European Convention or one of many UN accords.

The notion of international law is not new. It has existed in something like its present form since the end of World War II. Prior to 1945, the phrase "international law" referred simply to the mediation of relations among states, not to their domestic behavior. The great English jurist William Blackstone defined offenses against international law as the violation of safe conduct passes, the mistreatment of ambassadors, and piracy.

The foundation of the United Nations and the Nuremberg trials substantially widened the definition of international jurisdiction. But the real revolution has come since, and largely as a consequence of, the end of the Cold War. In 2001, Henry Kissinger made a startling observation:

> In less than a decade, an unprecedented concept has emerged to submit international politics to judicial procedures. It has spread with extraordinary speed and has

not been subject to systematic debate, partly because of the intimidating passion of its advocates. . . . The danger is that it is being pushed to extremes which risk substituting the tyranny of judges for that of governments; historically, the dictatorship of the virtuous has often led to inquisitions and even witch-hunts.

Kissinger was right. There has been a huge growth in international criminal law since the fall of the Berlin Wall. The process started when President George Bush Senior proclaimed a "new world order" on September 11, 1990. What he meant was that United Nations Security Council resolutions could be enforced by means of military force, since the East-West division in Europe and the hostility between the United States and the USSR had been overcome and the deadlock in the Security Council lifted. The United Nations would henceforth be able to call on its members to fight wars on its behalf, thereby giving international law a coercive quality that it had never had before.

The phrase "new world order" did not originate in the United States, though. It had been reintroduced into political discourse by the outgoing Soviet president, Mikhail Gorbachev, who rekindled the old Trotskyite dream of world government by calling for global governance and a unification of the world economy. Sure enough, institutions soon proliferated at an international level pursuing an overtly anti-conservative agenda and transferring ever more power away from ordinary people into obscure and unaccountable international institutions.

The change was put well by a prosecutor at the Yugoslav War Crimes Tribunal, Louise Arbour, who said in 1999, "We have passed from an era of co-operation between states into an era in which states can be constrained." The sentiment may be noble, but it immediately prompts the question: "Who is to check the powers of the person doing the constraining?"

Until the 1990s, international law consisted essentially of treaties between states. States were free agents that concluded contracts with one another. Occasionally, they created large institutions such as the United Nations to oversee the terms of their agreements, and occasionally the terms of the treaties were based on appeals to universal values such as the Conventions on Genocide or Torture. But none of these treaties gave rise to systems of coercive law comparable to the national law of a state, enforced by the police and the courts. Any penalties imposed for treaty violations were accepted voluntarily by the states that had signed them.

Moreover, to the extent that international treaties created obligations, those obligations concerned only states, not individuals. The Genocide and Torture

Conventions, for instance, require *national* bodies to pursue persons suspected of these crimes.

The big exception to this general rule was, of course, the European Union. The EU differs from all treaty organizations in that its law penetrates into the very fabric of national life by imposing obligations on individuals. The European treaties do not simply bind their signatories as states; they create a superior legal order, binding on individuals, and directly enforceable by national courts, with or without implementing legislation by the national legislatures. This is why the EU's power is so awesome. Once the new world order was proclaimed, the EU model was copied by other international bodies, and soon a host of international organizations had cropped up that claimed the right to regulate the most intimate details of people's lives.

The main vehicle for this internationalization of law has been the doctrine of "universal human rights." In the name of statements of desirable general principles, international organizations have been created that claim the right to interpret and even to enforce those principles as they see fit. People often react favorably when they hear that a new body has been created to protect human rights. What they perhaps do not realize is that ordinary people do not get any new rights as a result. What happens is that those working in the new institutions get to determine what our rights are. We may disagree with them, but we can do nothing about it, as no one elects them.

The European heads of state and government signed the European Charter of Fundamental Rights at the Nice summit in 2000. Initially, it had no legal base, since the European Constitution that would have authorized it was rejected in referendums in France and the Netherlands in 2005. But the EU went ahead anyway and created a new Human Rights Agency in Vienna, which was belatedly regularized when the Constitution came into effect in December 2009.

The Agency's remit is huge: the Charter of Fundamental Rights contains rules on everything—on the right to life, on liberty, on the right to a fair trial, and on the right to a family. There are rules on data protection, consumer protection, environmental protection, freedom of thought, freedom of religion. There is "the freedom of the arts" and "the right to education." Asylum policy, multiculturalism, social security, health care, the right to vote—you name it, the EU has a policy on it. There is even a "right to good administration"—which is pretty rich, coming from Brussels.

The EU is only one international body that claims the right to make and enforce laws. The Council of Europe, a pan-European organization that includes Russia, Ukraine, and other former Soviet republics, is home to the European Court of Human Rights in Strasbourg. Although separate from the EU, this organization has become the de facto Supreme Court for the whole of Europe. People with a grievance can pursue cases against their own national courts and national legislatures and obtain rulings from the ECHR made by judges who have nothing to do with their country; who do not have to bear the consequences of their own decisions; and who, in some cases, worked for the judiciary under communism.

The very existence of international courts like the ECHR violates the principle of territorial jurisdiction. According to this ancient doctrine, on which the rule of law is based, the rulings of judges are themselves embedded in the overall institutions of a state. They are governed by carefully drafted laws, and the national legislature and local authorities monitor the effect of these laws on society. So if a law gives rise to a judicial ruling whose effects are deemed unnecessarily expensive to society and its taxpayers, or detrimental in any other way, then the law can be changed. However, once international courts and international conventions become involved, this key link between national policy, the law-making process, and law enforcement is broken.

It was on these doctrines, and on this growing corpus of precedent, that the International Criminal Court was established, with the power to prosecute individuals, including heads of state and government, directly.

While Barack Obama has so far made no move to sign the ICC statute, his administration's body language is easy enough to read. In March 2009, in a closed meeting of the Security Council, Ambassador Susan Rice declared that the ICC "looks to become an important and credible instrument for trying to hold accountable the senior leadership responsible for atrocities committed in the Congo, Uganda, and Darfur." A week later Ben Chang, spokesman for National Security Advisor General James Jones, took a similar line, telling the *Washington Times*: "We support the ICC in its pursuit of those who've perpetrated war crimes."

Their comments were prompted by the ICC's decision to arraign, for the first time, a serving head of state, Sudan's Omar al-Bashir. Now Bashir is, by any definition, an unutterable swine. Having seized power in a military putsch, he maintained himself in office by displacing and terrorizing millions of his citizens. Some 300,000 Sudanese are estimated to have been killed in his civil wars and, while the government does not bear sole responsibility for each of those deaths, it must be reckoned the worst offender.

None of this, though, detracts from the most important aspect of the case, namely that Sudan *is not a signatory to the ICC treaty*. By applying an accord to a country that has not ratified it, the court is overturning three hundred years of jurisprudence, trampling over the notion of territorial jurisdiction and introducing the hugely dangerous idea that contracts can be enforced against legal persons who have declined to sign them.

You doubtless will have spotted the implications. The United States has (quite rightly) refused to accept the jurisdiction of the ICC. True to their history, Americans would rather place their trust in elected representatives than in global judges. Their congressmen believe (again, rightly) that signing the convention would open the door to a flood of mischievous claims, not only against U.S. servicemen, but also against their political leaders.

But even if the United States continues to remain outside the ICC, can you be certain that the precedent established in 2009 will not be extended? The technocrats at The Hague now presume to apply their writ where they please. Never mind national sovereignty, never mind representative democracy, never mind natural justice: All that matters to our transnational elites is power.

Here we reach the ICC's basic design flaw: Dictators will ignore it. Free democracies will no doubt allow themselves to be bullied over whether they are treating asylum seekers fairly, whether barring women from the army constitutes a human rights violation, whether a morning paper round amounts to the exploitation of children. But the real tyrants—and Bashir is a pretty good example of the genre—will react to such rulings not just by refusing to recognize them, but by digging in deeper, knowing that they can no longer expect to stand down and escape incarceration.

The ICC, in short, entrenches autocrats and weakens democrats. Its adoption represents the supreme example of the tendency described in this chapter: policy made in order to show that you're a nice guy rather than to effect practical improvements on the ground. That this administration should support the ICC is the ultimate proof of its European credentials.

7

WE THE PEOPLE . . .

> To preserve our independence, we must not let our rulers
> load us with perpetual debt. We must make our election
> between economy and liberty, or profusion and servitude.
>
> —THOMAS JEFFERSON, 1817

In the early summer of 2009, I was invited to the Army and Navy Club in Washington, D.C., to deliver "A British Response to the Tea Parties." Being British I of course said "right-oh," or something to that effect. Then I sat down and started Googling frantically to find out what the devil these Tea Parties were.

I should perhaps explain that, when covering U.S. affairs, British journalists tend to take their cue from the American left. At that stage, most of the big American media outlets were treating the Tea Party Movement as a non-story; so, naturally, British correspondents were ignoring the phenomenon altogether.

When I eventually found some references to the Tea Party Movement, they were almost all slighting. The protestors, I read, were disgruntled rednecks who couldn't bring themselves to accept that a mixed race president now occupied the White House. Or else they were dupes, who were being manipulated by cynical K Street lobbyists. Or perhaps they were a combination of the two.

The original Boston patriots were written off in similar terms. They were said to be a mob of "vagabonds, jack-tars, and disorderly Negroes." Or else they were dupes, who were being manipulated by cynical plotters around Sam Adams. Or perhaps they were a combination of the two.

These days, of course, we know better. The Boston protesters of 1773 are recognized more or less for what they were: the vanguard of a popular movement that embodied the spirit of a nation.

Their twenty-first-century heirs certainly see themselves in a similar light. And, while it is always easy to mock someone else's pretensions, they might just have a point.

It is already becoming hard to recall how total the defeat of conservative America appeared at the end of 2008. It wasn't just that the Republican Party had been trounced at every level. It was that a consensus appeared to have formed around a set of policies that, just twelve months earlier, would have been regarded as way to the left of what either party would consider acceptable.

The bailouts and nationalizations had expanded the federal government by nearly a third. Taxation, expenditure, and borrowing were all rising exponentially. Federal officials were presuming to tell private firms how to operate, even what to pay their employees. And, most shockingly of all, the entire nation appeared to be going along with the new dispensation.

Appearances, however, can be deceptive. Not for the first time, the political class had rushed to a consensus without carrying the rest of the country. Pundits and legislators, determined to look as though they were in charge of events, decreed stimulus after stimulus, bailout after bailout. But when the opinion polls started coming in, a very different picture emerged. According to a Rasmussen poll taken at the end of May 2009, only 21 percent of Americans supported the bailing out of General Motors, with 67 percent opposed. And if the car workers got little sympathy, the bankers who were blamed for causing the crisis in the first place got even less.

Not for the first time, what the French call the *pays légal* (the business, media, and political elites) had become divorced from the *pays réel* (everyone else). The governors had lost touch with the governed.

It is not a new phenomenon. Edmund Burke, the grandfather of British conservatism (and a friend, as we shall see later, to the cause of the American colonists) described it with matchless eloquence in 1790:

Because half a dozen grasshoppers under a fern make the field ring with their importunate chink, whilst thousands of great cattle, reposed beneath the shade of the British oak, chew the cud and are silent, pray do not imagine that those who make the noise are the only inhabitants of the field; that, of course, they are many in number; or that, after all, they are other than the little, shriveled, meager, hopping, though loud and troublesome, insects of the hour.

Burke, a conservative in every sense, disliked mass protest movements. Sympathetic as he might have been to the oxen, he became nervous at the thought of them stampeding. But America was founded in a popular uprising, and the modern Tea Party patriots were in no doubt that they represented the majority.

Events would largely vindicate their view. During the summer of 2009, the Tea Partiers changed the parameters and assumptions of public discourse in America, dragging politicians back to the concerns of the majority. The Obama administration had begun with broad public sympathy: Many Americans who resented the tax level, fretted about the deficit, and loathed the idea of state-run health care were nonetheless prepared to give their leaders the benefit of the doubt. But this sympathy evaporated as it started to become clear that the political class represented no one but itself.

It was a popular movement, not a political party, that formed the opposition to Big Government. The Republicans were following, rather than leading, public opinion. Having gone along with the expansion of the state under George Bush, they started to recover their nerve. Having, in most cases, supported the Bush stimulus package, they unanimously opposed the Obama follow-up.

During this time, watching closely from abroad, I noticed a change in tone. The Republicans were de-emphasizing many of their core messages. They weren't talking very much about guns, or abortions, or crime, or gays, or immigration, or foreign policy. In fact, they weren't really talking about much at all except tax cuts. And you know what? It worked.

On January 20, 2010, the Republican candidate won the Massachusetts Senate seat vacated by the death of Ted Kennedy. There was, of course, a pleasing symbolism in a popular anti-tax movement carrying the day in the state that contains Boston and Bunker Hill, Concord and Lexington. But there was, perhaps, a more immediate symbolism in the Republicans taking a seat that had been owned by the Democrats since John F. Kennedy's victory more than fifty-seven years earlier. A state with arguably the most left-wing electorate in the United States voted convincingly against the universal health-care scheme that had been Ted Kennedy's lifetime ambition. You didn't have to be a swivel-eyed anarcho-capitalist to feel that the federal government was expanding too far and too quickly. The people of Massachusetts took the level-headed view that the money was running out and, as in 1773, they spoke for the nation.

When I say that the Republicans were following public opinion rather than leading it, I mean it in no slighting spirit. All successful political parties do the same.

There are limits to what a group of politicians can achieve. It is asking too much of a party simultaneously to create public demand for a policy and to position itself as the beneficiary of that demand. I have lost count of how many times despairing British voters have asked, "Why can't you Tories make the case for tax cuts/ immigration controls/less bureaucracy/getting powers back from Brussels?"

The truthful answer, feeble as it sounds, is that politicians are not regarded as disinterested. When a political party makes the case for a policy, it is assumed to be grubbing for votes. When a non-political organization makes exactly the same case, people are disposed to give it a hearing.

American Republicans have enjoyed one great advantage over British Conservatives (and, for that matter, European Christian Democrats): They are part of a wider conservative movement. A party that is just one element—and not always the most important element—, of a broader family will always be in a stronger position than one that is expected simultaneously to perform the role of pressure group, newspaper, think tank, and election-winner.

Viewed from abroad, the existence of a vibrant conservative alliance is one of the most distinctive features of the American political scene. The rise of such a movement, beginning in the middle years of the twentieth century, accompanied and facilitated the rise of the Republican Party.

The first element in this conservative coalition was the think tank. Free-market institutes are now so ingrained into the conservative coalition that it is hard to imagine life without them. But, not so long ago, the left, entrenched as it was in universities, dominated the intellectual sphere.

Until the 1950s, conservatives lacked a philosophy. They had instincts, beliefs, policies, but nothing that could properly be called an ideology. This changed as think tanks began to play the role on the right that universities were playing on the left. Think-tankers didn't just write the script, or at least parts of the script; many of their script-writers become producers and directors when the Republicans took office and looked to fill their administrations.

It is hard to overstate the impact that small-government institutes have had on American politics. I am not just talking of the great foundations in D.C.: Heritage, Cato, the American Enterprise Institute, and the like. Every state in the Union now has at least one significant conservative think tank, many of them—the NCPA in Texas, Hoover in California—with as much national influence as the Washington titans. Wherever there is a legislature, there is a free-market think tank applying the doctrines of Hayek and Rothbard to local conditions.

Such organizations have given the right a philosophy every bit as internally consistent and comprehensive as the other side's. During the first half of the twentieth century, there was a widespread belief that intellect and progressive politics went hand-in-hand. Conservatism was not an ideology, but an amalgam of instincts: patriotism, religious faith, distrust of officialdom, and so on. This made it, in the most literal sense, a reactionary movement: a response to someone else's doctrine, not a doctrine in its own right.

Of course, many on the left still think this way, and see conservative intellectuals as class traitors. But this view no longer strikes a chord with the wider electorate, and serves only to make its advocates seem remote and self-righteous.

While think tanks played an important part in the air war, there was a ground war to be fought, too. And it is here that the conservative movement has most impressively come into its own. The Republican Party could never have succeeded had it not been surrounded and supported by organizations that were ideologically committed to kindred causes: gun clubs, home-school associations, local radio stations, evangelical churches. These bodies didn't simply provide foot soldiers: They were able to advance the agenda in a way that a politician couldn't easily do without coming across as self-interested.

What's more, these organizations recognized their shared interests. The last time I was in D.C., I spoke at the Wednesday Meeting run by Grover Norquist's Americans for Tax Reform. Here, gathered under one roof, was Hillary Clinton's "vast right-wing conspiracy": vaster, indeed, than I had ever imagined. Think-tankers rubbed shoulders with congressional aides, contrarian columnists with right-wing academics, Ayn Rand devotees with anti-health-reform campaigners, Republican candidates with sympathetic businessmen. Although there were many ideological and stylistic differences among those present, they were all there to advance a common cause. I kept thinking of Bismarck's remark about the German socialists: "We march separately, but we fight together."

The Tea Party Movement is the latest manifestation of this tradition: a popular *fronde* that is unaffiliated but conservative, political but skeptical toward political parties, angry but focused. You occasionally read that the Tea Parties were synthetic, that the crowds had somehow been artificially put together, that the rage was fabricated. In fact, the Tea Party phenomenon is an example of that rare beast, a genuinely spontaneous popular movement. One of its founders told me that it had started life as a twenty-two-person conference call, and had grown within weeks to an army of thousands.

There are limits, of course, to what such a movement can achieve. It has no legislators and can pass no laws. It has scant financial resources. Indeed, it has so far failed in its two main aims: to defeat the Obama health-care bill, and to reduce the levels of taxation and debt. But legislation takes place against a background of national debate and consensus, and this is what the Tea Partiers have helped to shift.

Just as there are limits to what a popular movement can achieve, so there are limits to what a political party can achieve. The Tea Party Movement is nourished by a very American creed, namely that governments don't have the answers, that reform comes from below, that people are wiser than their leaders. By taking their message directly to the streets, the Tea Partiers changed minds in a way that politicians couldn't. They have, in short, created an atmosphere in which candidates opposed to Big Government can win. Whether such candidates succeed, and whether they are able to effect a substantive change in public policy, will depend at least in part on what kind of relationship they retain with the wider movement.

During the middle years of the twentieth century, the left seemed to have won a permanent victory. The Democrats enjoyed what looked like a structural majority in the House of Representatives and, although Republicans could occasionally win the White House, they usually did so when they fielded deliberately nonpartisan candidates, such as Dwight Eisenhower.

The GOP leadership had accepted much of the Roosevelt settlement. Patrician, Northeastern, and fastidious, Republican bigwigs balked at the idea of mounting a populist challenge to the consensus. As the economist J. K. Galbraith put it in 1964: "These are the years of the liberal: almost everyone now so describes himself."

How did the party go from semipermanent opposition to mastery? The story was brilliantly told by two *Economist* journalists, John Micklethwait and Adrian Wooldridge, in their 2004 book *The Right Nation: Why America Is Different.*

They chronicled the transformation of the Republicans from an East Coast, preppy, country club party, a party of old money and big business, a party that kept losing, into an angrier, more church-going, more anti-government, Sunbelt party, a party that kept winning.

The story is epitomized by the history of the Bush family. Prescott Bush, George W.'s grandfather, was every inch an Establishment Republican: wealthy, well-connected, liberal, a stickler for good manners. A successful Wall Street banker, he represented Connecticut in the Senate between 1952 and 1963, and was well thought of for his bipartisanship, courtesy, and golfing ability.

His son, George H. W. Bush, did what many Americans of his generation were doing: He migrated South and West, leaving Yale for the tin-roofed oil town of Odessa, Texas. There he encountered a very different strain of Republicanism: more libertarian, more evangelical, and—in what was still a one-party Democratic state—more anti-Establishment.

By the time George W. Bush became governor of Texas, the transformation of the GOP was total. The forty-third president was almost exaggeratedly Texan in his speech and manner. Like their party, the Bushes had become more demotic, more anti-Washington, less interested in foreign affairs, and far more successful at the polls.

The family's migration from Kennebunkport to Crawford mirrored that of the GOP "from patrician to populist, from Northeastern to Southwestern, from pragmatic to ideological" as Micklethwait and Wooldridge put it.

Not all center-right parties have made this successful transformation. My own is still seen by many voters as the political wing of a closed Establishment: a party of black-tie dinners and private schools and gentlemen's clubs. It suffers electorally in consequence.

Indeed, by far the most successful Conservative over the past hundred years has been Margaret Thatcher, who aimed to transform Britain into a "home-owning and share-owning democracy." Perhaps her single most popular policy was to allow people who lived in houses owned by their local authorities to buy their own homes. The beneficiaries of that reform became her strongest supporters. But she was commensurately loathed by many of the upper class "Wets" who had previously run the Tory Party, and who regarded her radicalism as antithetical to everything they believed in. They were not bad people, the Wets. On the contrary, they generally were motivated by a belief in public service, by a high-minded (if pessimistic) patriotism, and by a touching sense of *noblesse oblige*. The trouble is that, like the 1960s Republicans, they kept losing: their modest, undoctrinaire conservatism couldn't be turned into a popular movement.

Only in very recent years has the British Conservative Party begun to adopt some of the ideas that brought success to the U.S. Republicans: the decentralization of power, referendums, recall mechanisms, school choice, and so on. Strangely enough, the leader who oversaw this change, David Cameron, is every bit as blue-blooded as the Bushes. Such are the paradoxes that make politics fascinating.

The transformation of the Republican Party had many elements, and we should be wary of oversimplification. But if there was a single policy that embodied the change, and began the party's revival, it was the embrace of localism and states' rights. The issue that catalyzed that change was the busing of schoolchildren, but that issue symbolized something much wider. A liberal elite appeared to have lost touch with the country. Leftist policymakers, who sent their own children to private or suburban schools, were imposing what seemed an unfair and disproportionate policy on everyone else, sometimes ordering their children to attend schools that were many miles away. When Ted Kennedy tried to remonstrate with an angry Irish-American crowd on the subject in Boston in 1974, he was chased into a federal building.

The Republicans saw their opportunity. They were no longer the elite. They could side with the ordinary voters against remote officials. They could take up the old Jeffersonian ideal that decisions should be taken as closely as possible to the people they affect.

Here was the formula that would secure their success: a success that was to reach its fullest flower in the victories of Ronald Reagan and, later, in the Contract with America.

Only now, perhaps, do we have the sense of perspective needed to appreciate the magnitude of the Contract. It wasn't just that Dick Armey and Newt Gingrich managed to win a congressional majority after forty years, turfing out a number of Democratic officeholders who had regarded their posts as permanent. It was that they then went on to prove that politicians can keep their promises.

The Contract took the form of a very short document: a series of eighteen simple, measurable promises, rounded off with the striking offer: "If we break this contract, throw us out." The Contract initially was scorned by Washington pundits. It was, they scoffed, far too concerned with such abstruse issues as internal congressional reforms. Out in the country, the columnists agreed, people were far more interested in bread-and-butter issues such as education and the economy.

But the Republican leaders had spotted something that the pundits had not. People were on the point of giving up on their politicians. A series of petty scandals had drained Congress of authority. Republicans grasped that, until it had put its own affairs in order, the House of Representatives would not be trusted with the affairs of the nation. The very first item of the Contract— "require all laws that apply to the rest of the country to apply equally to the Congress"—was dismissed by sophisticated correspondents. But, outside the Beltway, voters who had long given up on their representatives looked up with sudden interest.

Having cracked down on a number of congressional abuses, the representatives turned their attention outward, with legislation to balance the budget, tackle crime, and—outstandingly, as we have already seen—reform welfare.

I was so fascinated by the story of the Contract with America that I traveled to Atlanta to listen to Newt Gingrich, and to Dallas to discuss it with Dick Armey. When I asked them what the toughest part had been, both gave the same reply: "The toughest opposition comes from your own side."

When I returned, I set about selling the idea to my own party. During the 2010 general election, David Cameron posted 3.5 million copies of his Contract with Britain to targeted voters. It worked. He won.

The Contract with America was, as we can now see, the high point of anti-government Republicanism. As the party settled into office, it lost its hunger. As the years passed, the Republicans began to forget what had made them win.

Under the second Bush, the GOP began to drift toward big government, centralization, and crony capitalism. It reverted to the protectionism that had been its creed before World War II, imposing a steel tariff from no higher motive than to shore up support in a marginal state. It presumed to tell state legislatures what laws they should pass on moral issues, such as euthanasia and same-sex unions. It expanded the federal government's role in education. It pursued a vastly expensive foreign policy. It gave the security forces colossal new powers, some of them justified by the changed situation, but others wholly disproportionate. It pushed federal spending to unprecedented levels, while allowing the deficit to rise. Then, in its final days, it began bailing out, or seizing outright, failed businesses.

To put it at its simplest, the Republican Party started winning when it aligned itself with the masses against the elites, when it championed local prerogatives against Washington, when it stood for the individual against the state. It started losing when it reversed that alignment.

In the absence of an organized opposition party, Americans took opposition into their own hands. They took to the streets to remind their leaders of their duties under the Constitution. In doing so, they were living up to the highest American ideals, consciously emulating the eighteenth-century patriots whose creed they recited. A scheme to make America less American—less devolved, less independent, less competitive, less diverse, less free—provoked the rage of the American people themselves, or at least a goodly number of them.

For those of us who admire the American ideal, it was a heartening sight. After all, as the old chestnut has it, a democracy gets the politicians it deserves. Americans deserve better.

8

WHERE BRITISH LIBERTIES THRIVE

There is a straight road which runs from Runnymede to Philadelphia. We did not "borrow" provisions from the British Constitution, which had come from the people; those provisions were ours, paid for with the lives of our ancestors on many a battlefield. I have examined the matter. I tell you our Constitution came up from the body of a self-governing people. But we can lose our capacity to govern by its non-exercise.

—HATTON SUMNERS, 1937

You might be wondering why a patriotic British politician has written a book lauding the constitution of a state that was created out of a popular rising against Britain.

The answer is that, when I look at the United States, I see British liberties thriving. The men who made the Revolution didn't develop their doctrines in a vacuum. They were drawing on centuries of English political thought and, more to the point, political practice.

The ideas that animated the revolutionaries, and were eventually enshrined in the U.S. Constitution, were all commonplaces in contemporary British politics. Most Britons at the time would have assented cheerfully to the propositions that laws should be passed only by elected representatives, that taxes might not be levied save with the permission of the legislature, that no one should be subject to arbitrary punishment or confiscation, that ministers should be held to account by elected parliamentarians, that property rights should be defended by independent magistrates, and that there should be a separation between the executive, legislative, and judicial arms of the state.

American historians, quite understandably, tend not to emphasize the extent to which Britain sympathized with the grievances of the colonists. Later accounts of the revolution generally portrayed it as a national uprising—as, indeed, a War of Independence.

This interpretation, however, depends on a very selective reading of what the patriot leaders were arguing *at the time.* They saw themselves not as revolutionaries, but as conservatives. In their own minds, all they were asking for was what they had always assumed to be their birthright as Englishmen. The real revolutionaries, as they saw it, were those in the Georgian Court who were seeking to impose a new settlement, in contravention of the ancient constitution: one that would tilt the balance from legislature to executive, and open the door to oppressive government.

Obviously, once the fighting started, the patriot leaders began to use nationalist language in an attempt to rally as many colonists as possible to their cause. And, following their victory, they tended to stress this aspect of their cause, to reinterpret their recent past with one eye on where their actions had led. They would not have been human had they done otherwise. Nonetheless, the idea in 1776 that America was engaged in a war against a foreign nation would have struck most of the inhabitants of the colonies, patriot or loyalist, as bizarre.

In his 1999 study, *The Cousins' Wars*, Kevin Phillips approached the American Revolution more realistically, as a civil war within a common polity. More than this, he demonstrated that the Revolution was, in many ways, a successor to the English Civil War of the 1640s.

Those who had settled New England came largely from the Eastern counties of England. They built their houses in the East Anglian style, and named their towns after their ancestral homes: Hertford and Cambridge, Boston and Billerica. The English counties that they left behind became the heartland of the Parliamentary cause in the 1640s, Cromwell's Eastern Association.

When the fighting started in England, the New England Puritans began streaming back across the Atlantic to take up arms alongside their cousins. A majority of Harvard graduates in the year 1642 saw action with the Roundheads.

Virginia was a different story. Many of its colonists were from gentry families, and were often Episcopalian. Their family links were to the King's party, and they were far likelier to remain loyal to the Crown.

Phillips shows, by tracing genealogies, that the battle lines that were drawn in 1642 had not been rubbed away in 1776. Broadly speaking, those whose ancestors had fought for the Stuarts were likely to be loyalists; those who descended from the parliamentary side were likely to be patriots. The strongest supporters of the Revolution in North America, other than the New England Yankees, were the grandchildren of Ulster Protestants. When things were going badly for the Continental Army, George Washington declared bleakly, "If defeated everywhere else, I will make my stand for liberty among the Scots-Irish in my native Virginia."

Conversely, those likeliest to be Tories came, ancestrally, from what had been the Royalist parts of the British Isles: Northern and Western England, Wales, the Scottish Highlands, Catholic Ireland.

The rebel leaders were acutely aware of the link. They named their warships for Cromwell and Hampden, and drew consciously on the vocabulary of the earlier conflict, referring to American loyalists as "inimicals." George III, too, saw the connection, and spoke mournfully of the rebellion as "my Presbyterian war."

These same fault-lines can be seen in Britain at that time. Whigs, loosely descended from the Civil War

Roundheads, believed that the colonists had fair and reasonable grievances. Tories, heirs to the Civil War Cavaliers, argued that George III must assert his authority. London and the surrounding counties were broadly for the rebels, as were Lowland Scotland and the Puritan mill towns. The more conservative parts of the country, by and large, wanted the rising put down militarily. Ireland divided almost wholly along sectarian lines, Southern Catholics backing the King while Northern Protestants formed militia and drilled in imitation of their cousins in Virginia and Pennsylvania.

The greatest British parliamentarians of the age backed the patriot leaders. The American cause was virtually the only issue that united Edmund Burke, the father of modern British conservatism, with the Whig leader, Charles James Fox. The most famous speeches of that era came from British allies of the colonists.

"I rejoice that America has resisted," proclaimed William Pitt the Elder, setting out the case against the Stamp Act in 1766. "Three million people so dead to all feelings of liberty as voluntarily to submit to be slaves would have been fit instruments to make slaves of the rest [of us]."

"Let us get an American revenue as we have got an American Empire," said Burke in 1775, taking up the cause of no taxation without representation. "English privileges have made it all that it is; English privileges alone will make it all it can be."

When it became clear that the rebel cause was prevailing in 1780, Fox told the chamber, "If the ministry had succeeded in their first scheme on the liberties of America, the liberties of this country would have been at an end."

Such orations were almost certainly a truer indication of public sentiment than was the official policy of the ministry. We cannot measure contemporary public opinion by election results, since Great Britain at that time had an extremely restricted franchise. We can, however, make an educated guess on the basis of such quantifiable data as newspaper circulation, petitions delivered to Parliament (either for Coercion or for Conciliation), and the position of those few MPs who, under the Byzantine electoral rules that pertained until 1832, represented a broader section of the electorate. Extrapolating from these sources, historians have inferred that most of the population of Great Britain was in sympathy with the colonists. Indeed, the balance of opinion in the British Isles seems to have been similar to that in North America, with Tories accounting for perhaps a third of the population. The difference, of course, was that many more Americans had the right to vote, so the colonial assemblies were more representative of their populations.

When, in March 2010, I organized the inaugural British Tea Party in the fashionably liberal town of Brighton, some British leftists—and some puzzled Americans—asked why I was borrowing the symbol of a revolt against the British Crown. I reminded the audience of the state of public opinion in Britain in the 1770s. I spoke of the British heritage on which the original Tea Partiers had drawn. I recalled that the taxpayers' revolt that had sparked the American Revolution had begun on my side of the Atlantic: the cost of the Seven Years' War had pushed taxes up to 20 shillings for the average British subject, as against sixpence for the average colonist, and it had been the British government's determination to export at least part of this cost to North America that began the quarrel. Nonetheless, I added, we were not Americans: We would drink our tea, not dump it into the English Channel.

I don't recall this history in order to detract from the achievement of the American patriot leaders. It is true that Britain was halfhearted in its prosecution of the fighting. Many officers declined offers of command, and those who accepted fought dutifully rather than enthusiastically. It is true, too, that Britain had little appetite for the repression of its own kinsmen when there were more pressing battles to be waged against the Bourbon powers. Nonetheless, war is war, and there was something heroic about the willingness of the colonial leaders to take on what was already becoming the world's greatest military power.

I recount the narrative, rather, to stress a point that has often been missed by historians and politicians on both sides of the Atlantic. A common political culture encompassed Britain and America before and after the formal rupture. The two states drew on a common political heritage. Politicians on both sides of the Atlantic saw themselves as heirs to an inherited folkright of Saxon freedom, expressed in the common law. Both traced a direct political lineage back through the Glorious Revolution to the signing of Magna Carta in 1215. If anything, Americans placed (and place) greater store by that document than Britons. The site where Magna Carta was signed, at Runnymede in my constituency, went unmarked until 1957 when a memorial was erected there—by the American Bar Association.

It is no surprise, then, that amity was soon restored between the adversaries. When Britain formally recognized U.S. independence, John Adams became the first American minister to London. The speech he made, as he presented his credentials to George III, is so handsome and affecting that it is worth quoting in full:

> *Sir, the United States of America have appointed me their minister plenipotentiary to your Majesty, and have directed me to deliver to your Majesty this letter, which contains the evidence of it. It is in obedience to their express commands, that I have the honor to assure your Majesty of their unanimous disposition and desire to cultivate the most friendly and liberal intercourse between your Majesty's subjects and their citizens, and of their best wishes for your Majesty's health and happiness,*

and for that of your royal family. The appointment of a minister from the United States to your Majesty's Court will form an epoch in the history of England and of America. I think myself more fortunate than all my fellow citizens, in having the distinguished honor to be the first to stand in your Majesty's royal presence in a diplomatic character; and I shall esteem myself the happiest of men, if I can be instrumental in recommending my country more and more to your Majesty's royal benevolence, and of restoring an entire esteem, confidence, and affection, or, in better words, the old good nature and the old good humor between people, who, though separated by an ocean, and under different governments, have the same language, a similar religion, and kindred blood. I beg your Majesty's permission to add, that, although I have some time before been entrusted by my country, it was never in my whole life in a manner so agreeable to myself.

The king was visibly moved, and replied with a generosity that had eluded him during the recent conflict:

I wish you, sir, to believe, and that it may be understood in America, that I have done nothing in the late contest but what I thought myself indispensably bound to do, by the duty which I owed to my people. I will be very frank with you. I was the last to consent to the separation; but the separation having been made, and having become

*inevitable, I have always said, as I say now, that I
✓   would be the first to meet the friendship of the United
States as an independent power. The moment I see such
sentiments and language as yours prevail, and a disposi-
tion to give to this country the preference, that moment I
shall say, let the circumstances of language, religion, and
blood have their natural and full effect.*

And so, in time, it came to pass. The rapprochement
was not immediate. It took British Tories another generation to accept emotionally what they had accepted le-
gally: that America was truly an independent state. A
war—albeit an inconclusive and absurd war—was fought
before the British state was fully reconciled to its lost jurisdiction. Once this had happened, though, the way was
open to the Anglo-American imperium that has lasted to
our own day. Throughout the nineteenth century, the
Monroe Doctrine was made possible—enforced, we
might almost say—by the Royal Navy. And in the twentieth century, Britain and America fought side by side,
first against Prussian autocracy, then against Nazism, and
finally against Soviet Communism.

Those battles, and those victories, were not based
solely on "the circumstances of language, religion and
blood." They were based, even more, on a shared political heritage, an identity of culture and outlook.

Like other British MEPs, I am occasionally teased by Continental colleagues about the willingness of what they call "the Anglo-Saxons" to line up with the United States in foreign policy. Britain, they scoff, has turned itself into an American aircraft carrier. Do we have no foreign policy of our own?

Gently, I try to explain that, coming as we do from a common culture, we tend to react in similar ways when we face the same problems. We have a number of things in common, I tell them, we Anglo-Saxons. We try to see the other chap's point of view. We revere our laws and our parliaments. We bridle at injustice. We dislike bullies. We are slow—often too slow—to anger, but terrifying when roused.

As Kipling put it:

> The Saxon is not like us Normans. His manners are
> not so polite.
> But he never means anything serious till he talks
> about justice and right.
> When he stands like an ox in the furrow, with his
> sullen set eyes on your own,
> And grumbles, "This isn't fair dealing," my son,
> leave the Saxon alone.

To return to Kagan's metaphor, if Americans are from Mars, then the free English-speaking nations share the Martian orbit, rather than that of Venusian

Europe. Look at the countries that are first to deploy force alongside the United States and you see the same names coming up again and again: United Kingdom, Canada, Australia, New Zealand.

America doesn't have to choose between Europeanization and isolation. There is another option: the Anglosphere. Instead of pursuing harmonization as Europeans do—through rules and bureaucracies—we should prefer an organic and wholly voluntary association of free peoples. Instead of integration among states, let us have collaboration between individuals, businesses, and other bodies. Instead of a union of governments, let us pursue a union of values.

Until very recently, states were defined by their geographical location. In the post-war era, regional blocs seemed to make sense. The United States concerned itself with its hemisphere, as it had since the 1820s. Britain joined a European customs union. Australia and New Zealand took on responsibilities in the South Pacific.

Technological change, however, has rendered geographical proximity irrelevant. The Internet has made nonsense of distance. Capital now surges around the world at the touch of a button. It is as easy to sell to another continent as to the next county. Indeed, often easier. Businesses in my constituency generally are more comfortable dealing with Anglosphere firms—firms that share their language, common law system, commercial practices, and accountancy rules—than with businesses that happen to be in the EU.

The United States doesn't need to sign up to supranational structures in order to prove its internationalist credentials. It doesn't need to sacrifice sovereignty or democracy in order to participate in the comity of nations. It can, instead, seek to inspire by example, holding true to the precepts of its constitution, offering its hand to any nation that accepts those values.

Let me return, one more time, to Thomas Jefferson, a bust of whom stands on my desk as I write these words. Jefferson predicted that there would be a thick flow of settlers from the Old World to the New, and that few would choose to make the return journey. His prediction, of course, came true in a spectacular way. But it is important to be clear about the basis of Jefferson's confidence. He didn't think that there was a magical quality in American soil, or American water, or the American gene pool. (He did, slightly eccentrically, tell a French friend, "Our sky is always clear, that of Europe always cloudy," which statement one can attribute either to patriotic exuberance or to a radically different eighteenth-century climate.) Rather, he believed that the genius of America lay in its system of government, and that any country that ordered its affairs along republican principles could be as happy and prosperous as the United States.

Encouragingly, Barack Obama made precisely the same argument on the night of his election victory in

Chicago: "Tonight we proved once more that the true strength of our nation comes not from the might of our arms or the scale of our wealth, but from the enduring power of our ideals: democracy, liberty, opportunity, and unyielding hope."

Quite so. Which is why the rest of us want you to cleave fast to those ideals. They have served to make you rich and free, to the benefit of other nations as well as your own. And you will perhaps allow me a certain additional pride, as a British politician, when I say that your ideals came from ours, that the highest conception of British liberty was committed to paper in the old courthouse at Philadelphia.

Which brings me to my country's present discontents. The fears that the American patriot leaders had about a Hanoverian tyranny were, in retrospect, exaggerated. The United Kingdom did not develop into an absolutist state. Power continued to pass from the Crown to the House of Commons. Indeed, many of the political developments that occurred in the United States happened in parallel in the United Kingdom, for the obvious reason that the two states were starting from a similar place.

The real divergence has come much more recently. It has come about as a result of a general shift in power in the United Kingdom from Parliament to quangos, from local councils to central bureaucracies, and, most damagingly, from Westminster to the EU. It is the process of European integration, above all, that has concentrated power in the hands of functionaries, in Whitehall as well as in Brussels. With every new European Directive, every Regulation, Britain is tugged away from its Martian orbit by the gravitational pull of Venus.

In consequence, the grievances which the Americans laid against George III are now, more than two centuries later, coming to pass in earnest. Colossal sums are being commandeered by the government in order to fund bail-outs and nationalizations, without any proper parliamentary authorization. Legislation happens increasingly through what are called Standing Orders: a device that allows ministers to make laws without parliamentary consent—often for the purpose of implementing EU standards. Elections have been drained of purpose, and turnout is falling. Local councils have surrendered their prerogatives to the central *apparat*. Foreign treaties are signed by the Prime Minister under what is known as Crown prerogative, meaning that there is no need for parliamentary approval. Appointments to the growing corpus of state functionaries—the quangocracy—are made in the same way.

How aptly the British people might today apply the ringing phrases of the Declaration of Independence against their own rulers who have "combined with others to subject us to a jurisdiction foreign to our constitution, and unacknowledged by our laws."

Throughout my career in politics, I have campaigned to apply Jeffersonian democracy to British political conditions, to recover those British freedoms that have flourished more happily in America than in their native soil. Ever since my election, I have worked to repatriate our revolution. So you can imagine how I feel when I see the United States making the same mistakes that Britain has made: expanding its government, regulating private commerce, centralizing its jurisdiction, breaking the link between taxation and representation, abandoning its sovereignty.

The United States is an ideal as well as a country. As John Winthrop told his shipmates on the way to the first settlements in 1630:

> We shall find that the God of Israel is among us, when ten of us shall be able to resist a thousand of our enemies; when He shall make us a praise and glory that men shall say of succeeding plantations, "may the Lord make it like that of New England." For we must consider that we shall be as a city upon a hill. The eyes of all people are upon us.

The eyes of all people are upon you. And if they see you repudiate your past, abandon that which has brought you to greatness, become just another country, they, too, will have lost something.

So let me close with a heartfelt imprecation, from a Briton who loves his country to Americans who still believe in theirs. Honor the genius of your founders. Respect the most sublime constitution devised by human intelligence. Keep faith with the design that has made you independent. Preserve the freedom of the nation to which, by good fortune and God's grace, you are privileged to belong.

INDEX

Page numbers of illustrations appear in italics.

INDEX

About the Author

Daniel Hannan is a writer and a politician. He contributes to several newspapers, including the *Wall Street Journal* and the London *Daily Telegraph*. A former president of the Oxford University Conservative Association, he was elected to the European Parliament in 1999, at the age of twenty-seven, and has been reelected twice.